winter trails™
trails
COLORADO

Help Us Keep This Guide Up to Date

Every effort has been made by the author and editors to make this guide as accurate and useful as possible. However, many things can change after a guide is published—new products and information become available, regulations change, techniques evolve, etc.

We would love to hear from you concerning your experiences with this guide and how you feel it could be improved and be kept up to date. While we may not be able to respond to all comments and suggestions, we'll take them to heart and we'll make certain to share them with the author. Please send your comments and suggestions to the following address:

The Globe Pequot Press
Reader Response/Editorial Department
P.O. Box 833
Old Saybrook, CT 06475

Or you may e-mail us at:
editorial@globe-pequot.com

Thanks for your input, and happy travels!

winter trails™

COLORADO

The Best Cross-Country Ski
& Snowshoe Trails

by

TARI & ANDY LIGHTBODY

The
Globe
Pequot
Press

OLD SAYBROOK, CONNECTICUT

Winter Trails is a trademark of The Globe Pequot Press.

Cover photographs: © Gary Brettnacher and Adventure Photo & Film, inset photo: © Brad Johnson and Adventure Photo & Film.
Cover and text design: Nancy Freeborn
Trail maps created by Equator Graphics © The Globe Pequot Press
State map: Lisa Reneson

Library of Congress Cataloging-in-Publication Data
Lightbody, Tari.
    Winter trails Colorado : the best-cross country ski & snowshoe trails / by Tari and Andy Lightbody. — 1st ed.
        p. cm. — (Winter trails series)
        ISBN 0-7627-0303-2
        1. Cross-country skiing—Colorado—Guidebooks.   2. Snowshoes and snowshoeing—Colorado—Guidebooks.   3. Cross-country ski trails—Colorado—Guidebooks.   4. Colorado—Guidebooks.   I. Lightbody, Andy.   II. Title.   III. Series.
    GV854.5.C6L54 1999
    917.8804'33—dc21   98-38869
                                                                CIP

Manufactured in the United States of America
First Edition/First Printing

Dedication

This book is dedicated to our four great children who often went "in tow" along with us to visit the many areas and trails, and to Ray and Betty Lightbody for helping watch "The Rugrats" when it required long writing sessions.

To the kids:

Daniel "where's the double black diamonds" Lightbody

Jeffrey "where's the snowboard trails" Lightbody

Matthew "uh, I have just one question to ask you," Lightbody

Jennifer "how do I look?" Lightbody

To the Grandparents:

Betty "I'm in charge here" Lightbody

Ray "It's okay with me, but go ask your Grandmother" Lightbody

To Everyone—Thank You!!

Winter Trails: Colorado

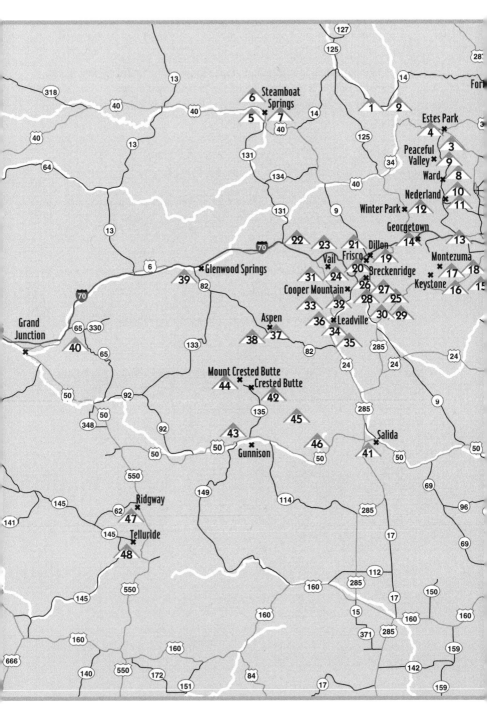

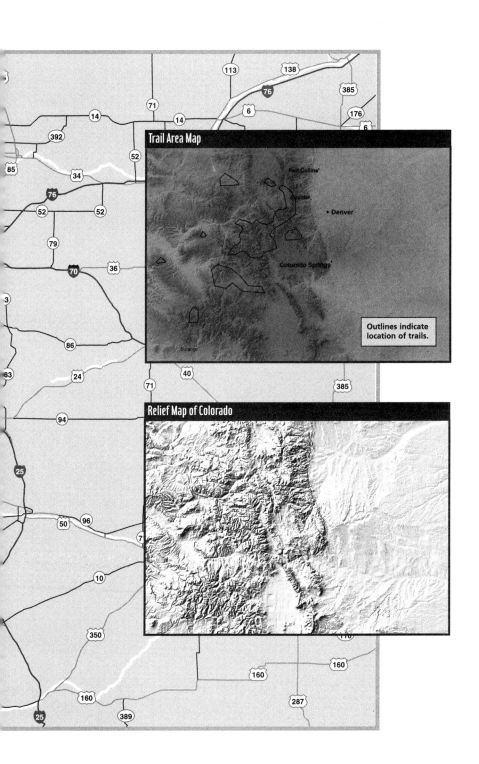

Trail Area Map

Fort Collins

Boulder

• Denver

Colorado Springs

Durango

Outlines indicate
location of trails.

Relief Map of Colorado

Contents

Acknowledgments

Winter Trails: Colorado could not have been compiled and written without a lot of input, direction, suggestions and assistance from those individuals, organizations, associations, state and federal agencies and ski resort/destination companies that have and continue to work so hard to make Colorado the premier state for winter outdoor recreation.

Our special thanks to the following: The 10th Mountain Hut Division Association; The San Juan Hut Systems; The Monarch Ski Resort and Monarch Mountain Lodge; The Mesa Lakes Resort; Powderhorn Ski Resort; Copper Mountain Ski Resort; The Keystone Ski Resort; Summit County Chamber of Commerce; The Loveland Ski Resort; Estes Park Resort Chamber Association; The Sunlight Mountain Ski Resort; Angela Glenn, Douglass Caldwell, Ty Hall and the folks at the Tennessee Pass Cookhouse; Columbia Sportswear; Yana Havaty, James Saunders, Francie MacCarty, Leigh Girvir Yule, Ken Swift, Scott Peterson, Gina Kroft and Crested Butte Mountain Resort; Holly Resignolo and the Great Divide Lodge in Breckenridge; Jim Felton and Leigh Pezzicara of the Vail Resorts group; Atlas Snowshoe; the U.S. Forest Service and all its dedicated Rangers; the Bureau of Land Management and all of its dedicated officers; and all the chamber offices, ski resorts and "dedicated" winter sports enthusiasts who took us in tow and worked so hard to give us a first-hand appreciation for the thousands of cross-country ski and snowshoe trails that grace our state.

A special thanks also to Martin Fox, Jennifer Radden, and Kelly Allen of MapTech for introducing us to the TopoScout CD-Rom map system. Their line of high-quality topographic maps on computer CDs are not only ideal for everyone who loves the outdoors and wants to know how to get there, but their technology made writing this book the easiest and most exact where-to-go guide we've ever written!

And a special thanks to the Magellan Corporation for making and providing easy-to-use, easy-to-understand and extremely exacting high-technology Global Positioning Satellite (GPS) hand-held receivers. This tool will never replace the North Pole, but it's an instrument for outdoorspeople that's much more precise than a compass for navigating both on and off the roads, the trails, and the beaten paths. Our personal thanks and appreciation to Dennis Phillips from the Walker Agency for bringing this technology to us.

Introduction

In our writing careers, which between the two of us totals close to 40 years, *Winter Trails: Colorado* has to rate as one of the most challenging books we've ever written. The problem lies in the fact that Colorado has so many great cross-country ski and snowshoe trails for the backcountry explorer that trying to sort through the thousands of trails and adventure areas was a most daunting task. Unlike other states, where the cross-country ski and snowshoe trails are predominantly found to be perfectly groomed and almost always in and around ski areas and their companion Nordic centers, the trails in Colorado often offer the outdoorsperson true backcountry adventures and experiences.

Many times restaurants, overnight accommodations, and even convenience stores are located miles away from the trails. And although the trails presented here range from the Beginner/Novice all the way through to Advanced/Expert levels, the underlying theme and caution is *if you backcountry ski or snowshoe anywhere in the Rocky Mountains, you must be self-sufficient and plan to be self-reliant.*

Trail Selections and Ratings

Trails that are highlighted in this book are some of the best that you'll find anywhere in the state of Colorado. They're also some of the best that you'll find anywhere in the country! They are not, however, always the most popular or famous trails for cross-country skiing or backcountry snowshoeing. Although many of the trails are well traversed, the routes we present represent a complete spectrum and variety of trails, for all levels of skiing/shoeing abilities. We selected some of the trails simply because they are not the most popular—translating to a better quality outdoor/backcountry experience: fewer crowds, unspoiled scenery, and plenty of solitude.

Many of the trails profiled in *Winter Trails: Colorado* are found in areas where there are countless other trails that wind, intersect, and meet up with the profiled route. Nordic centers, ski areas, and locals in all of these areas are likely to have "their" favorite trails as well. Visiting the area where a trail is profiled will likely lead you to other "favorites" of your own. The nice thing about Colorado is that there are many great trails for just about every skiing/shoeing ability.

Photo by Sport Obermeyer, courtesy of Aspen Skiing Company

Ten years ago, snowshoeing as a recreational sport was in its infancy. Downhill and cross-country skiing in Colorado were the rage with just about everyone. Today, skiers and shoers are found in the backcountry in unprecedented numbers. Everyone from the beginner, looking for a casual wilderness stroll, to the expert, craving a real aerobic workout, are all on the trails!

As you read through *Winter Trails: Colorado,* pay close attention to how each of the trails is classified: Beginner/Novice, Intermediate, or Expert/Advanced. The **Beginner/Novice trails** are designed to be relatively easy, for those who are first-timers or who have limited trail experience. These trails are the ones that are relatively short in mileage/duration and usually can be accomplished in a half day or less. They also are ones that are well marked/signed, have relatively flat terrain, mild ascents and descents, and grade levels of 10 percent or less.

The **Intermediate trails** are suited to those who have some backcountry trail experience and are comfortable with their abilities to ski or shoe both on and off the beaten path. The trails are longer in mileage/duration and can take four hours to a full day to accomplish. These trails are designed for skiers/shoers who have good map-reading skills, allowing them to navigate through an area, are not intimidated by having to "break" or blaze their own trail, and are seeking more challenging terrain in terms of ascents and descents—with grades of 20 percent to 30 percent or more.

The **Advanced/Expert trails** are just that! They are designed for skiers/shoers with lots of backcountry experience and abilities. These trails are long in mileage/duration and most will take anywhere from 5 hours to several days to complete. They are designed for those with appropriate equipment and excellent backcountry winter survival skills. These trails have grades of from 30 percent to over 50 percent.

Our best advice is to ski or shoe at your own personal ability level. Don't try to be a hero and think you can just "go for it." That's a dangerous decision that will get you into trouble in a hurry! Select trails that are below or equal to your skill level. It's always a pleasant journey to select a trail that leaves you fulfilled and with great memories. It's a nightmare to discover too late that you overestimated your abilities and are now scared to death that you are possibly in real danger.

For any trails with prolonged climbs of a 30 percent or steeper grade, we strongly advise using snowshoes designed for extreme backcountry conditions.

Altitude Acclimation

Cross-country skiing and snowshoeing on the trails in the backcountry of Colorado require the ultimate in self-reliance. Let's begin with a basic: If you're not accustomed and acclimated to the high-altitude conditions found in the state, you're liable to put your health at risk and jeopardize your high mountain adventure or expedition.

If you're not already a Colorado resident and acclimated to the high elevations, and if you drive or fly into any of the Front Range areas of Colorado, you're going to need a little time to adjust to the Rocky Mountain high. Keep in mind, that even before you head up into the mountains, you're already about 1 mile above sea level. Enjoying all of *Winter Trails: Colorado* means that for cross-country skiing and snowshoeing, everything is up from there.

Unless you're already acclimatized and used to the high-altitude climbing, skiing, and trekking that's required to enjoy *Winter Trails: Colorado,* you may want to spend the day of your arrival to the area getting in "sync" with much higher than sea level altitudes. There's a lot less oxygen to breathe in the mountains. As we like to tell visitors to the area, "It's beautiful up here, but bring your own air!" Jumping from at or near sea level to the Colorado Rocky Mountains can easily bring on a case of altitude sickness.

The chronic symptoms of altitude sickness include headache, nausea, tiredness, and other symptoms that are much like a case of the flu. Doctors at the Denver Health Medical Center say that 60 percent of people will suffer from a mild to severe case of altitude sickness by traveling at or above 8,000 feet. A variety of supposed cures—such as taking aspirin, vitamins, and various herbs—are always being touted, but results vary widely from person to person. Best bet is to spend the first day taking it easy. Get plenty of rest, drink plenty of liquids, avoid alcohol, and keep your physical exertion to a minimum. Some doctors recommend that you might want to get a prescription for a small individual bottle of oxygen. It can help.

If you start to suffer from altitude sickness, you're going to have to slow down, or you're going to be miserable. Remember oxygen, rest, and plenty of liquids are about the only way to combat the effects of altitude sickness, short of coming down to a lower elevation.

Equipment and Survival Gear

Equipment for cross-country skiing and snowshoeing has changed radically over the past few years. It's not that the older equipment isn't good, but the new high-tech equipment being introduced is often lighter, stronger, and more versatile than what was offered even 5 years ago.

Snowshoes almost always have built-in grips on the bottom of the shoes for climbing and traction. Cross-country skis for Colorado are going to require what are called *skins;* they're traction devices that are either glued or strapped onto your ski's bottom surface so that you can literally "get a grip," while climbing upward. Without them—on both waxless and waxable skis—you're going to find that the climbs are much more difficult, if not impossible. Although there are a lot of different types of skis that work well in the backcountry, the best are sturdy mountaineering types with metal edges.

Because just about all the trails are loaded with lots of up and down climbing or gliding, a good set of ski or shoe poles is another must. Although regular commercial fixed-length downhill poles will suffice, the best and most practical for backcountry adventures are the poles that are adjustable and convertible to probe poles, which are used for locating avalanche victims. We hope you'll never need them to fill this function, but it's always best to be prepared.

If you're new to the world of cross-country skiing and snowshoeing, it's probably best to rent your equipment the first few times you go out. This way you can sample a variety of makes, models, styles, and offerings from a host of different makers and manufacturers. Once you decide what you like and what fits your style, then it's time to make a purchase. Ski shops, resorts, and Nordic centers throughout the state rent equipment for everything from a half day to a week or more. Some even will work a package deal on rental equipment for the entire season.

Popular ski brands for cross-country and backcountry skiing in Colorado include Fisher, Karhu, Tua, and Rossignol. Popular brands of snowshoes include Redfeather, Little Bear, Tubbs, Atlas, Sherpa, Baldas, and TSL. The last five also design shoes for extreme, steep backcountry terrain.

Because so many of the backcountry trails are remote, and often times groups of skiers/shoers can get spread out over a mile or more of trail, you might want to consider taking along small portable two-way radios. The latest introductions from Motorola are lightweight, moderately priced, and have a range of several miles. In our gear bag, these radios are considered must equipment, allowing us to stay in contact with everyone in the group.

Selecting the right clothing for your backcountry adventures is of paramount importance. As with the ski and shoe industries, the revolution in clothing for the winter enthusiast has resulted in a host of lighter weight, warmer, water-resistant, and breathable miracle fabrics. Volumes could be written on the subject of clothing only. Suffice it to say that in

Colorado, the weather is predictably unpredictable. You can literally get up in the morning with a bright blue sky and moderate temperatures only to get out on a backcountry trail and have a foot or more of snow blast down on you in an hour. If you're not dressed for all of these conditions, you're going to end up having a cold, wet, and miserable outing—at best. At worst you could be in real danger of suffering from hypothermia and even dying.

It's been said about Colorado, "If you don't like the weather in Colorado, wait five minutes. It will change." Probably the best way to dress for the trail is by wearing layered clothing—clothing that can be added to or taken off as the weather conditions change. Make sure that the clothing is breathable, that it will allow body moisture to be wicked away from your skin and escape out of the clothes. As you trek or ski, you're going to work up a sweat. The secret to staying warm is to stay dry and comfortable. Hats, scarves, balaclavas, and gloves are a must.

Because weather conditions and trail conditions can change so quickly, you'd be foolish if you don't prepare and carry with you a complete winter survival kit. At minimum this should be a backpack or fanny pack loaded up with the gear you might need to survive in the wilds on your own. The following are some of the items that should be considered a must each and every time you hit the trail:

1. Fanny pack or backpack
2. 1-quart water bottle
3. Gaiter or rain suit
4. Emergency space blanket
5. Sunglasses/lip balm/sunscreen
6. Map of the area and compass, preferably even a handheld GPS receiver
7. High energy food—enough for an overnight stay. . . . just in case
8. Waterproof matches, fire-starting material
9. Knife/multipurpose tool
10. First-aid kit
11. Tin cup or aluminum pan to melt snow
12. Flashlight with extra batteries
13. Headlamp
14. Avalanche locator beacon and probe poles
15. Lightweight but sturdy snow shovel

16. Extra clothing

17. Hunter's plastic orange tape—great for marking an unknown trail or route

18. Pencil and paper

19. Plastic whistle

Other items that you might want to include are emergency signal flares, smoke signaling device, a first-aid book, survival manual, and even one or two common automobile road flares. Road flares are waterproof, easy to light, and burn at such an intense heat level that they are ideal for starting even wet kindling for your fire.

If you're planning an overnight excursion, additional items to add to your pack should include the following:

1. Foam pad—Thinsolate, Therma-Rest or other waterproof type

2. Water filter

3. Sleeping bag in waterproof cover

4. Ground tarp

5. Bivvy sack

6. Tent with extra cord

7. Extra batteries for lights and radios

Photo by Tari and Andy Lightbody

Trip Planning and Trail Safety

While the Rocky Mountains of Colorado are some of the most beautiful mountains in the entire world, they are also some of the most challenging. Even Beginner/Novice trails have a higher caution and danger factor than going out and taking a couple of laps on the snow-covered flat track at the local Nordic center. This is not to say that cross-country skiing and snowshoeing in the state is dangerous and should be avoided. Quite the contrary is true if you are properly clothed, equipped, and have properly planned for your backcountry adventure.

Trails and the accompanying maps in *Winter Trails: Colorado* are to be used as guides only. Exact routes and conditions will vary greatly on a regular basis because of use, weather conditions, trail conditions, etc. Signs that were bright, new, and easy to see this year could have been knocked down, weathered, or victimized by squirrels and porcupines by the time you encounter them! It's best to make sure that you have current and detailed maps, the latest avalanche information, a compass, and even a GPS receiver. It's also of paramount importance that you know how to read a map and use the compass and GPS for exact navigation in the backcountry.

Probably one of the greatest modern inventions/tools for the outdoor enthusiast is the Global Positioning Satellite (GPS) handheld receiver. Developed as a military instrument for U.S. troops around the world, a GPS receiver allows a person on the ground to be able to locate the latitude and longitude coordinates anywhere on the planet by putting them in touch with a system of twenty-four satellites now in orbit. Precise to less than 100 yards in exact positioning, the GPS coordinates can help you (if you know how to read a map with latitude/longitude coordinates) navigate in the backcountry. Keep in mind that GPS receivers often don't work or receive signals well when you are in a heavy canopied forest, so readings should be taken when you are on the top of a hill or in an open area.

For those who do not possess those skills, you'd better learn them! Check with local ski shops, ski resorts, Nordic centers, Forest Service, Park Service, etc. and get the latest information before you get on the trail. If you're venturing to an area that is unfamiliar to you, you may want to inquire about hiring a guide. Again, most all of the ski resorts and Nordic centers have a variety of tour packages and guides available.

Summer trails are usually well marked and well worn. In the winter they can be covered with deep snows and visibility can be severely limited. The old adage, "if you get lost in the woods, hug a tree and wait for help," may be good for summer backcountry adventures, but it likely wouldn't be sound advice if you're lost in the winter. Being lost in winter—with or without a blizzard dumping on you—can be a very frightening experience. You had best be prepared to navigate your way to safety or at least into an area where mountain search and rescue teams can locate you.

Beginning with the basics: Make sure that somebody knows where you are going, how long you are supposed to be gone, and when you are to return. That way, if you're not back when you're supposed to be, somebody can notify the proper authorities and get help organized and on its way to you.

Also be aware that these major search and rescue operations can cost tens of thousands of dollars in manpower hours and equipment. In Colorado every skier/shoer should consider it another "must" to purchase a Colorado Conservation Certificate. It costs only 25 cents and is good for the year. For a quarter you've just purchased the best and cheapest insurance policy of your life! If you have a valid Colorado Conservation Certificate (CCC) you are automatically covered and protected against any and all costs incurred in all search and rescue operations. Without it the state of Colorado will still rescue or assist you with whatever emergency has happened, but then they are going to bill you for those emergency costs!

In addition to the concerns about weather, there is—even on the trails with a low avalanche danger rating—the possibility of snow slides. Unfortunately it's a fact of life that goes along with rugged, wild, and high mountains. Each year there are hundreds of avalanches throughout the state. Some are small and hurt no one. Others are massive and result in injury and death to skiers, shoers, climbers, snowmobilers, and hikers. The best way to handle avalanches is to avoid them! That may sound silly and simplistic, but it's the best safety advice anyone can offer you.

Always check on avalanche/snow slide dangers before you go out on any of the trails. The state of Colorado maintains a twenty-four-hour-a-day Avalanche Information Center that provides recorded and constantly updated information about all areas of the state. You should call them at (970) 668–0600 each and every time before venturing out.

Avalanche locator beacons, probe poles, and avalanche shovels are items you must have with you at all times. When you take an organized tour or hire a snow-country guide, such gear is considered mandatory. The best high-tech unit available comes from a Colorado-based company called Back Country Access (800–670–TREK). If you're looking for topline shovels and other equipment, you might want to get a catalog from Life Link (800–443–8620).

Here are a few safety tips to always keep in mind about avalanches in the backcountry:

1. Danger of avalanche or snowslides increases greatly on any slope with an angle at or over 30 degrees.

2. It is always safer to ski or trek along the edge of angled open areas, than it is to venture out into the center.

3. Snow stability changes on a daily and sometimes hourly basis. Snow is most stable when skied or trekked in the early morning when it's still icy and crusty. Snow becomes less stable when there are conditions of fog and when skiing in the late morning, midday, and late afternoon.

4. New snow on top of old snow is often very unstable and unsettled. Wait a day or two after a snowstorm while the sun and warmer temperatures help stabilize the new snow as part of the existing snow pack.

5. Cornices that are wet and dripping should be avoided from both above and below. If you're walking out on them, they can break and take you with them. If you're underneath and it breaks free, it can bury you instantly.

6. When crossing a potential avalanche chute or danger area, never cross as a group. Only one person at a time should cross the area and then radio or hand signal back to the rest of the group for the next person to come across. This way, if there is a snow slide, others in the party will be safe and can conduct the rescue operation.

Back-Country Etiquette

Backcountry cross-country skiing and snowshoeing is one of the fastest growing segments of winter outdoor recreation. It's relatively low tech and low impact and is a great way to get out and see the majestic beauty that can be found in the high country. With the record numbers of people on the trails in the winter, comes the concern about being able to share the pristine lands with all winter users while protecting the fragile environment now and for generations to come.

Whether you are a long time resident of Colorado or a visitor, keep in mind that nobody owns the trails. They literally do belong to everyone, and for this reason everyone has a responsibility to protect them from abuse and misuse. Remember, if you're strong enough to pack all your supplies in with you, you should be strong enough to pack out your trash! Everyone is a steward for the beauty that the backcountry offers.

We hope you enjoy the magnificence of the Rocky Mountains as we have. We wish you the best for years of outdoor winter recreation and safe journeys.

We look forward to seeing you on the trails!

Key to Icons

cross-country skiing trail

snowshoeing trail

skate skiing (skating) trail

colorado

Photo by Tom Stillo, courtesy of Crested Butte Mountain Resort

Lake Agnes Cabin

Lake Agnes Cabin, Colorado State Forest, Ft. Collins, CO

Type of trail:	▬▬▬ ⬤⬤⬤
Also used by:	Snowmobilers and snowboarders
Distance:	7.0 miles
Terrain:	Short trail but steep enough to provide challenging uphill hike to Cabin, and then great downhill run back to trailhead.
Trail difficulty:	Intermediate to advanced
Surface quality:	Ungroomed, but often ski/snowshoe tracked.
Elevation:	The trailhead is at 9,686 feet and the hut is at 10,360 feet.
Time:	3 to 5 hours
Avalanche danger:	Low, but some avalanche terrain is encountered.
Snowmobile use:	Low
Food and facilities:	Whether you're planning on day touring only or staying over at the Lake Agnes Cabin, it's best to get all your groceries, gas, snacks, water, etc. before you leave the Ft. Collins area. There are a lot of small roadside gas stations, a few cafes, and a few motels along Highway 14, but for the most part they are closed during the winter.

The Lake Agnes Cabin is operated by the Colorado State Parks group, and reservations for using the cabin are required in advance. For further information about availability, call (800) 678–2267. Rental costs for the cabin range from $35 to $50 per night depending on weekend and holidays, so it's best to call for exact prices. The cost for the overnight stay is for your entire group, however, and represents a real bargain! There is also an additional $2.00 charge per person for what is called a "walk-in" fee for use of the cabin either overnight or for day use.

Located within the 70,000 acres of the Colorado State Forest, the popular trail to Lake Agnes is short but offers steep enough grades to be considered very challenging and carries a rating of intermediate to advanced in terms of skier/snowshoer ability. Not designed for the beginner, this trail represents a ready challenge to the experienced backcountry skier or snowshoer. Running through dense forests and crossing a logging camp, the trail provides so many types of terrain that when you make it to the cabin, you will be ready for a well-deserved rest before exploring the surrounding slopes.

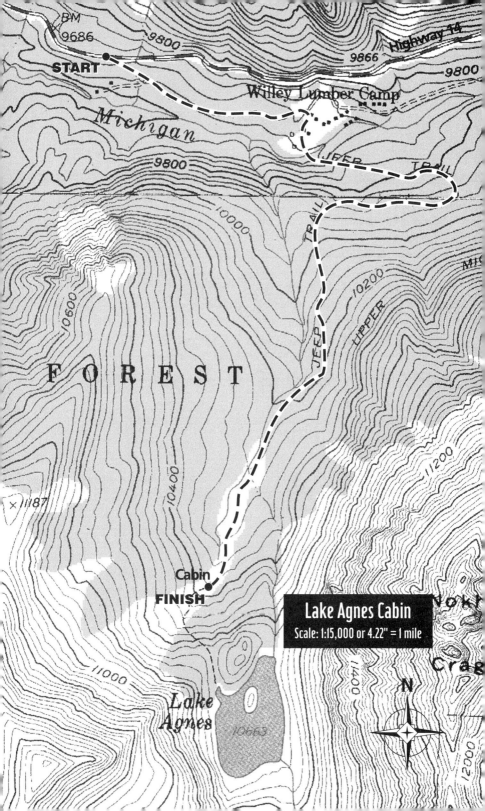

BM
9686
9800
START
Highway 14
9866
9800
Willey Lumber Camp
Michigan
9800
JEEP
TRAIL
TRAIL
10000
MIS
10200
10600
UPPER
JEEP
FOREST
× 11187
10400
11200
Cabin
FINISH
Lake Agnes Cabin
Scale: 1:15,000 or 4.22" = 1 mile
Nok
11000
Crag
Lake
Agnes
10663
N
11400
12000

The cabin itself is operated by the Colorado Division of Parks and Outdoor Recreation and can accommodate up to six people for an overnight stay. A wood-burning stove supplies heat, and you obtain water by melting snow, so day users, please don't bring any dogs.

From the Lake Agnes trailhead, head southeast on the four-wheel-drive road, crossing over a creek and climbing and dropping over a series of steep grades through a thick canopy of trees. Up- and downhill grades are often 30 percent to 50 percent as soon as you leave the trailhead, so plan on using skis with skins and shoes with poles. At about the 0.5-mile point, you'll encounter a sharp curve that veers to the south. You'll then see a fork in the road. Head right into a clearing of the Willey Lumber Camp at about 0.75 mile from the trailhead. Although your elevation has changed very little, you've in fact already climbed and descended about 500 feet in just under 1.0 mile.

You then head back into the forest, veering southeast around a tight curve that ultimately takes you west in a stretch of less than 0.5 mile. The road then turns to the south, climbing more steadily. In this 1.5-mile stretch, you'll gain upward of over 900 feet in elevation. Although the grades aren't radical, they are constant. The last 0.5 mile takes you southwest along the Lake Agnes drainage and to the cabin, which you'll see on the south side of a high-elevation meadow.

Directions at a glance

- The trailhead/gate to Lake Agnes is well marked with a parking area on the south side of Highway 14.
- Go through the gate and ski/shoe approximately 0.75 mile to the east to the Willey Lumber Camp.
- Take 4-by-4-vehicle road out of the Willey Lumber Camp to the southeast. Look for signs to Lake Agnes.
- Continue skiing/shoeing south another 2.5 miles along the Lake Agnes drainage.
- The Lake Agnes Cabin will be found along the drainage area on the south side of the trail.
- To return follow the same route back to the trailhead.

From the cabin it's just under another 0.5 mile to Lake Agnes. It is however all uphill with grades of from 16 percent to 28 percent. However once you reach the lake, it's a great open area with a lot of downhill runs and trails. The area is becoming popular with snowboarders, who trek in on shoes and then switch to boards once they reach the lake. After an afternoon of exploring, it's a fast trek or glide back down to the cabin or all the way back down to the trailhead. Steep and slow ascents up the trail to the cabin make for a wild ride back down the trail when it's time to head home!

How to get there

From Ft. Collins take U.S. 287 north to the junction of Colorado Highway 14. Go west on Highway 14 for approximately 60 miles to Cameron Pass. The trailhead to Lake Agnes trailhead is 2.5 miles west of Cameron Pass. The parking area is on the south side of Highway 14. To reach the trailhead, ski or snowshoe past the gate 0.5 mile to the entrance of the Colorado State Forest. Follow the road to the Willey Lumber Camp and then right onto a summer four-wheel-drive road marked for Lake Agnes.

Zimmerman Lake

Fort Collins, CO

Type of trail:	▬▬▶ ⬬
Distance:	3.0 miles
Terrain:	Short trail with smooth and steady ascent to Lake and fairly gentle back to the trailhead.
Trail difficulty:	Novice to intermediate
Surface quality:	Ungroomed, but often ski/snowshoe tracked.
Elevation:	Trail starts at 10,020 feet and ends at 10,495 feet.
Time:	2 to 3 hours
Avalanche danger:	Low, but the areas surrounding Montgomery Pass have avalanche hazards.
Food and facilities:	It's best to get all your groceries, gas, snacks, water, etc. before you leave the Ft. Collins area. There are a lot of small "roadside" gas stations, a few cafes, and a few motels along Highway 14, but for the most part they are closed during the winter. Once you get onto the Zimmerman Lake trail, there are no facilities.

Because of the steep slopes and rocky ridges of the Montgomery Pass and Cameron Pass areas, the early winter snows stick, and skiing or snowshoeing starts as early as November. The Zimmerman Lake Trail, which is popular with the locals, is a short excursion from the main road into a heavily forested area. Offering a mostly smooth, steady ascent, it has only two steep sections, one right as the trail begins and the other soon afterward at about the 0.25-mile point. Resting at the foot of cliffs that form the northern border of the Neota Wilderness Area, Zimmerman Lake offers a peaceful, solitary setting unencumbered by the mechanized traffic created by snowmobiles.

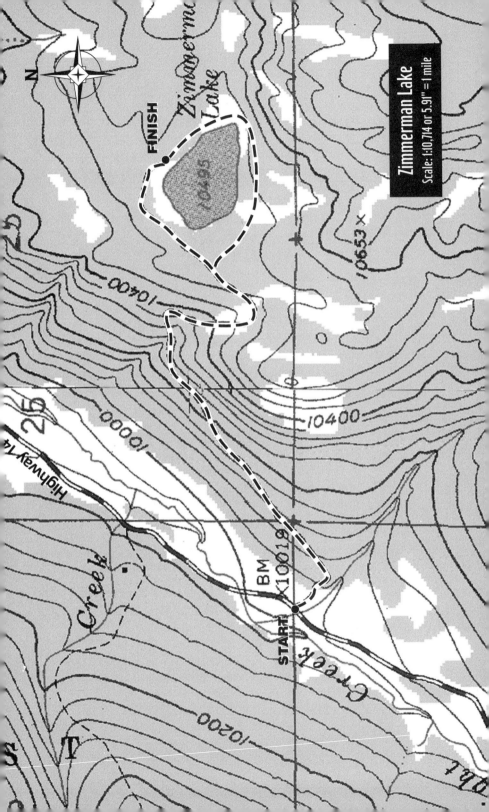

Zimmerman Lake

Zimmerman Lake
Scale: 1:10,714 or 5.91" = 1 mile

N

FINISH

10495

10400

10653 ×

10400

10000

Highway 14

25

Creek

BM
×10019

START

Creek

10200

S T

494

From the trailhead use the old road at the south end. Starting at an elevation of 10,020 feet, the trail heads southeast and climbs through a spruce/fir forest, switchbacking in a slight zigzag direction that sends you to the northeast. Before you've gone the first 0.25 mile, the trail drops almost 100 feet in elevation into a low saddle before climbing in a steep 20 percent grade up to about 10,500 feet. It levels off for a short stretch, dips again, and then climbs near the 1.0-mile point, gradually climbing the rest of the way. A little after the half-way mark, the trail bends to the south for several hundred yards and then turns to the northeast again to round the northern edge of Lake Zimmerman.

Once you get to the lake, you may want to extend your trip by using the 1.0-mile-long Loop Trail, which goes around the lake. This loop intersects the Meadows Ski Trail near the dam on Zimmerman Lake, and the Loop Trail can be easily skied or trekked in either direction. When it's time to head back to the car, just follow the same route you used coming in.

How to get there

From Ft. Collins take U.S. 287 north to the junction of Colorado Highway 14. Go west on Highway 14 for approximately 58 miles. Approximately 2.25 miles before you reach the top of Cameron Pass, pull off at the Zimmerman Lake parking area on the east side of the road.

Directions at a glance

- The trailhead to Zimmerman Lake begins at the parking lot.
- Trail follows the road to the southeast and goes 0.25 mile, then drops down steeply, and then climbs steeply for an eighth of a mile.
- Trail levels and then climbs gently the rest of the way to the lake.
- Return to the trailhead back the same route you used to come into the area.

Alternate route

- If you want to extend your ski/snowshoe route, pick up the Loop Trail at Zimmerman Lake.
- Route can be traveled in either direction and totals another 1.0 mile.
- Use same route to ski/shoe back to the trailhead.

Bear Lake

Rocky Mountain National Park, Estes Park, CO

Type of trail:	▬▬ 🔘
Also used by:	Ice fishermen
Distance:	0.75-mile loop around Bear Lake; 3.5-mile round-trip to Nymph, Dream, and Emerald Lakes.
Terrain:	Loop around Bear Lake is flat and gentle. Trail to Nymph, Dream, and Emerald provides steady but gentle ascents.
Trail difficulty:	Novice to intermediate
Surface quality:	Ungroomed, but often ski/snowshoe tracked.
Elevation:	Trail starts at 9,400 feet and ends at 10,230 feet.
Time:	30 minutes to 1 hour around Bear Lake loop 2 to 3 hours roundtrip to Emerald Lake
Avalanche danger:	Low
Food and facilities:	While the Rocky Mountain National Park is a popular winter destination, there are not a lot of facilities open in the park during the cross-country skiing and snowshoeing season. Outside of restroom facilities at the Bear Lake area and the Park's Visitor Center, the closest food and overnight accommodations will be found in the town of Estes Park, which has plenty of grocery, convenience stores, gas stations, and places to get lunches and snacks before heading into the park. For Rocky Mountain National Park information, call (970) 586–1206. It costs $10 per vehicle to enter the park, but after that there are no additional charges for using the winter recreation areas and trails.

The Estes Park Chamber Resort Association can provide skiers/shoers with brochures and referrals on lodging and restaurants. Call toll-free at (800) 44-ESTES (37837).

The premier hotel in Estes Park is the Stanley Hotel. Built in 1909 by Mr. F. O. Stanley—the inventor of the Stanley Steamer automobile—the historical and elegant hotel has been remodeled and renovated within the last couple of years. It's pricey, but grand.

Established by Congress in 1915, the Rocky Mountain National Park is 265,727 acres of spectacular mountain scenery, including one of the "Fourteeners"—Longs Peak at 14,255 feet. In the park you might see elk, deer, and an occasional moose. During the winter months, great horned owls and stellar jays make the park their home. Located on the

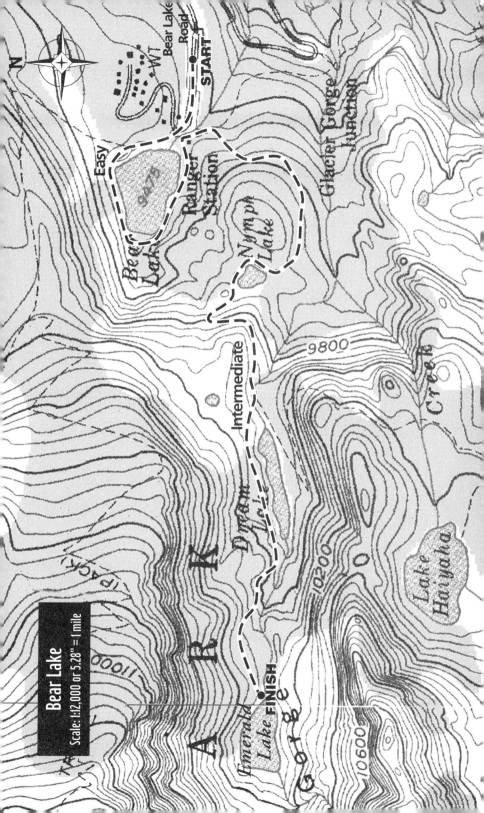

east side of the Continental Divide, the park is a convenient distance for winter enthusiasts from Denver and the Front Range. Snowmobilers are only allowed in on the west side access from Grand Lake and can travel on Trail Ridge Road up around Milner Pass. Snowmobile traffic is not permitted on the cross-country and snowshoe trails described here.

The route to Bear Lake is short with only a moderate and steady climb. If the pristine views aren't enough of a reason to venture forth, then take your fishing pole and ice auger. Ice fishing at Emerald Lake can reap cutthroat, rainbow, and brown trout. Check with the park ranger for limits and regulations.

From the parking area near Bear Lake, head north across the road and look for the well-marked trailhead. The "quickie" and easiest route is a short trail up to Bear Lake and a loop around. Taking less than one hour and covering just over 0.75 mile, it's perfect for you if you are a novice skier/snowshoer. On weekends this area is pretty crowded, but if you come on weekdays, you can enjoy much more solitude.

A short distance after starting up to Bear Lake, a trail cuts off that will take you the half-mile south of Nymph Lake. Gaining 225 feet in elevation, the trail is also rated as easy. It heads south before forking. Take the right—or west—route, which soon winds around to the southwest and leads you to the small lake.

The trail that goes on from Nymph Lake to Dream and Emerald Lakes is rated as moderately difficult and climbs about 300 feet in elevation. From the west shore of

Directions at a glance

- The trailhead for Bear Lake begins at the parking area and is well signed.

- Follow the signs up 0.25 mile and follow the trail around the lake. It's only 0.75-mile loop around Bear Lake, which brings you back to the trailhead.

Alternate route

- Follow the trail from parking lot toward Bear Lake. Less than an eighth of a mile from trailhead, take the route that will direct you to Nymph, Dream, and Emerald Lakes.

- Route to Nymph Lake is approximately 0.5 mile and is rated as easy.

- From Nymph Lake the trail to Dream Lake and Emerald Lake is rated as intermediate.

- Trail from Nymph Lake to Dream Lake covers approximately 0.5 mile and climbs steadily, gaining about 300 feet in elevation.

- Trail from Dream Lake to Emerald Lake is well signed and covers another 0.5 mile with a steady climb to around 10,300 feet.

- To return to the trailhead, enjoy a gentle glide or trek back along the same route.

Photo by Rob Gracie, courtesy of Aspen Skiing Company

Nymph Lake, head north on a switchback that will take you finally to the west. Keep on the right side of the gully, climbing steadily 0.5 mile to Dream Lake.

If Dream Lake is frozen solid, you can ski or snowshoe across but always beware that lake crossings are inherently dangerous. If the ice is too thin over the lake, head up the left side of the valley above the lake for several hundred yards. When the terrain levels, cross to the right side of the valley through the trees and continue on a little more than 0.5 mile to Emerald Lake at 10,230 feet.

How to get there

From Boulder head north and then northwest on U.S. Highway 36 approximately 31 miles to Estes Park. Drive through the town and follow Highway 36 signs to the entrance of the Rocky Mountain National Park at the Beaver Meadows entrance station. Pay your $10 per vehicle day-use fee there. After entering the park, stay on the main park road for 0.25 mile, then turn left onto the Bear Lake Road. Another 9.0 miles and it will bring you to the parking area east of Bear Lake.

Bear Lake to Fern Lake
Rocky Mountain National Park, Estes Park, CO

Type of trail: ▬▬ ⬤

Distance: 5 miles one-way to Fern Lake.
10 miles one-way to Moraine Park; shuttle vehicle required for return trip.

Terrain: Challenging climbs and descents all along the route.

Trail difficulty: Advanced/expert

Surface quality: First 2 miles are ungroomed but often ski/snowshoe tracked. Rest of trail is ungroomed backcountry conditions.

Elevation: Bear Lake trailhead is at 9,475 feet. Fern Lake is at 9,180 feet. Moraine Park trail end is at 8,200 feet.

Time: 2 days

Avalanche danger: Low to moderate. Avalanche chutes exist along the way and extreme caution should always be taken.

Food and facilities: While the Rocky Mountain National Park is a popular winter destination, there are not a lot of facilities open in the park during the cross-country skiing and snowshoeing season. Outside of restroom facilities at the Bear Lake area and the park's Visitor Center, you'll find the closest food and overnight accommodations in Estes Park, which has plenty of grocery, convenience stores, gas stations, and places to get lunches and snacks before heading into the park. For Rocky Mountain National Park information, call (970) 586–1206. It costs $10 per vehicle to enter the park, but after that there are no additional charges for using the winter recreation areas and trails.

If you're going to the trail from Bear Lake to Moraine Park, you're going to have to plan on leaving a shuttle vehicle at the end of the trail. Winter shuttle rides from Moraine Park can be arranged through the Estes Park Chamber Resort Association, but it's best to leave a shuttle car at the trail's end.

The Estes Park Chamber Resort Association can provide you with brochures and referrals on lodging and restaurants. Call toll-free, (800) 44–ESTES (37837).

The premier hotel in Estes Park is the Stanley Hotel. Built in 1909 by Mr. F. O. Stanley—the inventor of the Stanley Steamer automobile—the historical and elegant hotel has been remodeled and renovated within the last couple of years. It's pricey, but grand.

Bear Lake to Fern Lake
Scale: 1:40,000 or 1.58" = 1 mile

The Rocky Mountain National Park offers 415 square miles of untamed forests, valleys, and mountain areas for the cross-country skier and snowshoer. All are a relatively short distance from metro Denver and the Front Range. Even in the wintertime Moraine Park Campground is open for tent and RV camping, while the Longs Peak Campground, looking out over the 14,255-foot Longs Peak, is open to tent camping only. There's no firewood in the park, and campers must bring their own water. But an overnight adventure on one of the unmarked trails is truly worth the experience for skiers or snowshoers who are familiar with Colorado's temperamental weather conditions and are well versed in topographical map reading.

Winter camping gear, food, maps, compass, and a GPS receiver are a must for this route. This trail from Bear Lake begins as an easy hike or glide. But soon after skiing or snowshoeing off of the beginner route, the trail is long and difficult. Follow this path and the snow can become thin and slushy at the lower elevations, while remaining waist deep in the mountain passes.

The beauty and challenge of the Bear Lake/Moraine Park Trail lies in overnighting along the trail in the most primitive winter conditions. Although carving out an overnight snow cave is an option, preparing for a comfortable overnight winter stay with tents, sleeping bags, lanterns/flashlights, freeze-dried foods, and self-contained stoves and fire-starters can make it a most memorable overnight adventure trip.

Ski or snowshoe around the east edge of Bear Lake for about an eighth of a mile and turn north to intersect the Flattop Mountain Trail. You'll ski or snowshoe east over a flat switchback that'll steer you over a small hill dotted with aspens, until you are finally heading west (or to your left). About 0.50 mile from the trailhead, you'll ski/trek to the top of the ridge, contouring along a broad valley to the north and west, while staying on the right side of the stream.

Heading west continue on through the woods, passing a trail junction on your left at about the 0.75-mile mark. Veer to the right or northwest, steadily climbing. You can follow the summer trail, but some of it is on a steep slope and the snow cover is often poor. Continue to follow the basic route, but seek out the best trail. *Exercise caution:* There is some potential avalanche danger in the area. You should have avalanche beacons, shovels, and latest updates on potential avalanche slides.

At about the 2.25-mile point, you will reach Marigold Pond and then Two Rivers Lake to the south. From this point the trail is not well marked and topo maps and compass are a must. A handheld GPS receiver is a bonus to take you farther along the trail.

Directions at a glance

- The trailhead for Bear Lake begins at the parking area and is well signed.
- Go north an eighth of a mile on Bear Lake trail then right to intersect the Flattop Mountain Trail.
- At 0.5-mile mark the trail will turn left and start heading west.
- At 0.75-mile mark, take the trail to the northwest that's marked as the route to Marigold Pond, Two Rivers Lake, and Lake Helene.
- At about 2.5 miles, you'll reach the Marigold Pond, then Two Rivers Lake, and then Lake Helene. From this point topo maps and compass are necessary.
- Trail makes a hard right turn and treks north along the base of Joe Mills Mountain and along the edge of Odessa Lake.
- Ski/trek downhill for the next 1.0 mile, and you'll reach Fern Lake.
- Fern Lake is about the halfway point and a good area to set up your overnight winter camp.
- Follow summer trail marked to The Pool from the east side of Fern Lake.
- Trail routes downhill in a north and northeast direction along Fern Lake.
- Cross the Pool Bridge where Fern Creek and the Big Thompson River merge.
- Trail to the east for the next couple of miles following the signs to Moraine Park.
- Pick up the shuttle vehicle at Moraine Park and drive back to the Bear Lake trailhead to retrieve your other car.

If you want to do a little flat-ski skating or snow trekking, test the ice thickness on Two Rivers Lake, and if it's thick enough, ski or snowshoe around and across it. If you're dropping down low to the lake level, ski or shoe across it, heading west a short distance to Lake Helene.

After the fun on the "flat stuff," head to your right and north to Odessa Gorge. Climb the ridge between Odessa Gorge and Lake Helene for a short distance to the first small break in the ridgeline. Traverse to the right as you descend and look uphill to the top of Joe Mills Mountain to again assess the possible avalanche danger. Chutes abound in this area.

If it's safe, enjoy a thrilling downhill run. Once you're down, you'll see that the right side of the valley leads naturally to Odessa Lake at about 3.5 miles from the start of the trail.

Follow the narrow gorge, staying to the right of the streambed for the next 0.25 mile. Cross the stream, then follow it down to the left side, bending slightly away to the left as you do so. The terrain grows steep, and you can downhill one more time before the route curves to the east, or right, toward Fern Lake. If you want to stay overnight for your winter camping excursion in this area, the Fern Lake area is a lot less windy and more comfortable than Odessa Gorge.

After overnighting in the region of Fern Lake, you've got about a 5.0-mile ski/shoe trek that is mostly downhill. Following the summer trail with its excellent signage from the east side of Fern Lake, you'll drop quickly through a series of switchbacks that ultimately continue east to The Pool on the Big Thompson River with elevation drops of from 20 percent to 40 percent. Cross the Pool Bridge and continue on the trail for the last 3.0 miles, dropping steadily along the valley, following the signs to Moraine Park.

Reach the Moraine Park area and pick up the shuttle vehicle that you parked on the trail.

How to get there

From Boulder head north and then northwest on U.S. Highway 36 approximately 31 miles to Estes Park. Drive through the town and follow Highway 36 signs to the entrance of the Rocky Mountain National Park at the Beaver Meadows entrance station. Pay your $10 per vehicle day-use fee there. After entering the park, stay on the main park road for 0.25 mile and then turn left onto the Bear Lake Road. Another 9.0 miles and it will bring you to the parking area east of Bear Lake.

Service Creek

Service Creek State Wildlife Area, Steamboat Springs, CO

Type of trail:	▄▄▄▄ ⬤
Distance:	4.4 miles to 5.4 miles
Terrain:	Gradual, but continual ascents to end of trail and then gentle glide/trek back to trailhead.
Trail difficulty:	Intermediate to difficult
Surface quality:	Ungroomed backcountry conditions.
Elevation:	Trailhead 7,000 feet, climbs to 7,840 feet.
Time:	2 to 5 hours
Avalanche danger:	Low to moderate
Food and facilities:	Gas, food, drinks, and all equipment needs should definitely be taken care of before leaving Steamboat Springs. Very few towns and winter facilities are offered once you leave Steamboat Springs. Because you're going into a true wilderness area, everything has to be packed in, and you'd better plan on being totally self-sufficient.

Because the Service Creek State Wildlife Area (SWA) is so remote, for the latest conditions on snow, avalanche dangers, and road closures in the area, call the Stagecoach Park Service (970–736–8306).

For information about Steamboat Springs and adventures in the area, call (970) 879–0880 or contact the Web site: www.steamboat-chamber.com.

In the winter months the SWA is closed because it is a major wintering area for herds of Rocky Mountain elk and deer. No vehicles are allowed. However it is open to cross-country skiers/snowshoers looking for a pristine and uncrowded wilderness area that provides some great winter wildlife viewing.

Depending on where you have to park, follow the main road from the turnoff at County Road 18 at the SWA signs up the main road 0.5 mile to the Service Creek trailhead parking lot. This parking area is open to summer visitors but is closed during the winter.

The trail is very popular during the spring, summer, and fall, but nearly abandoned during the snow season. The isolation makes this a trail offering a great deal of backcountry beauty and the experience of skiing into a true wilderness area. Because all of the area beyond the trailhead parking lot is a designated wilderness area, there is no mechanized

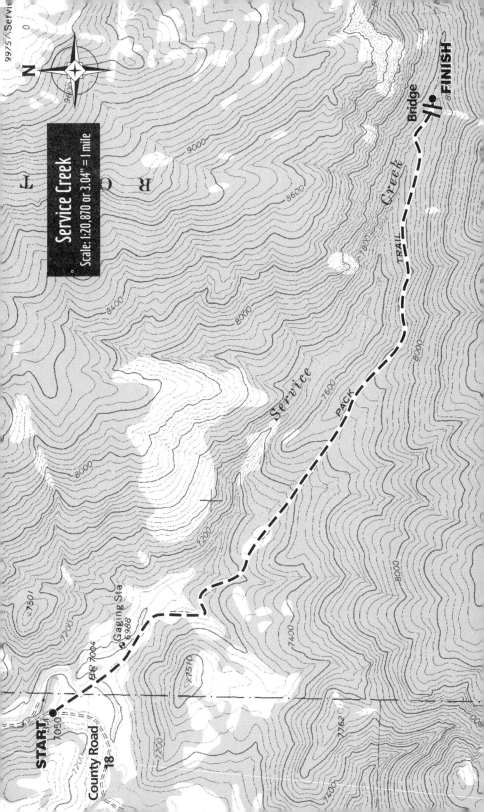

travel of any kind ever allowed. No snowmobiles, no ATVs, and not even mountain bikers are allowed in any season.

From the trailhead the route that is designated TR 1105 on USGS topographic maps immediately begins climbing steadily along the south side of Service Creek. Although rated at an intermediate ability level, this trail requires a lot of climbing and is recommended for the skier/snowshoer who's in good physical condition. The ancient forests of conifers are mature and grand and virtually untouched by man. The surrounding mountain views are pristine, and very much the way they have been for thousands of years. The beauty of this tour is unsurpassed. What makes it so inviting is that it is also short enough to make the excursion into the wilderness a one-day trip; you do not have to make it into a much more challenging overnight adventure.

At the 2.2-mile point, you'll come to an old bridge that crosses Service Creek. Skiers and shoers will find this is a natural spot to stop, rest, and take in the natural beauty and the deafening silence that surrounds you. Service Creek has more than a few small waterfalls that often freeze solid in the colder winter months. Cascading ice sheets and strange water sculptures can make for some great and very unusual photo opportunities. Hiking or skiing back out from this point is a lot less physically taxing, and the downhill runs provide a much quicker trip back to the Service Creek trailhead.

How to get there

While there's a variety of roads and routes that will get you close to the Service Creek State Wildlife Area (SWA), the best

Directions at a glance

- Trailhead begins at the east end of the SWA parking lot that has wooden sign marked TR 1105. (Route will start at turnout if SWA parking lot is not cleared.)

- The trail climbs out of parking lot and continues on the south side of Service Creek.

- Follow the trail 2.2 miles to the old bridge that crosses Service Creek.

- Return by following the same route back downhill to the parking lot.

all-season route is to take Highway 40 south from Steamboat Springs approximately 2.0 miles to Highway 131. Then take Highway 131 about 10.0 miles south to County Road 14. Follow the signs toward Stagecoach Reservoir. Go south on County Road 14 approximately 6.0 miles, then take County Road 18 east. The County Road 18 turnoff will be on your left. Go past the Stagecoach Reservoir lower dam. If the road is plowed, it's another 1.7 miles to the Service Creek State Wildlife Area (SWA). The turnout is well marked and is on your right. If the road is not plowed, you can park at the dam and ski down County Road 18 to the SWA area.

Strawberry Hot Springs

Steamboat Springs, CO

Type of trail:	▬▬▬ ▦
Terrain:	Steep drop at the beginning, gradual climb along creek and steep climb out.
Distance:	6.0 miles
Surface quality:	Ungroomed backcountry conditions.
Trail difficulty:	Intermediate
Elevation:	Trailhead 7,200 feet, climbs to 7,400 feet
Time:	3 to 5 hours
Avalanche danger:	Low
Food and facilities:	Winter services in the area are sparse at best. Fuel up your vehicle, check your equipment, and purchase your drinks, sack lunches, and supplies before leaving Steamboat Springs. The city of Steamboat Springs has great restaurants, grocery/liquor stores, ski/snowshoe shops, and rentals, as well as plenty of motels and bed-and-breakfast accommodations. You can call for information about the city's offerings, as well as other ski/shoe adventures in the area at (970) 879–0880 or on the Internet at www.steamboat-chamber.com.

If you want to stay over at the Strawberry Park Hot Springs Resort, bring your sleeping bag and groceries; the resort has five rustic cabins and one converted railroad car caboose. All overnight accommodations are heated and there's a shared bath house and shower facility. Cabins rent for less than $50 per night, the caboose goes for $75 per night, and all sleep up to four adults. Unless you're staying overnight at the resort cabins, there is no overnight parking/camping in the lot. The cabins and the caboose accommodations are very popular so make reservations at least 30 days ahead. For information about the Strawberry Hot Springs Resort, call (970) 879–0342.

The trailhead begins at the resort parking lot and the trail is rated as intermediate. At the trailhead, the path will go for approximately 200 yards and then drop down into Hot Spring Creek. The terrain is steep and provides a good challenge if you are an intermediate level skier or shoer. It is steep for approximately 0.25 mile and then levels out at the bottom of the canyon. The trail stays on the north side of Hot Spring Creek and runs about 2.5 miles west to Mad Creek Village.

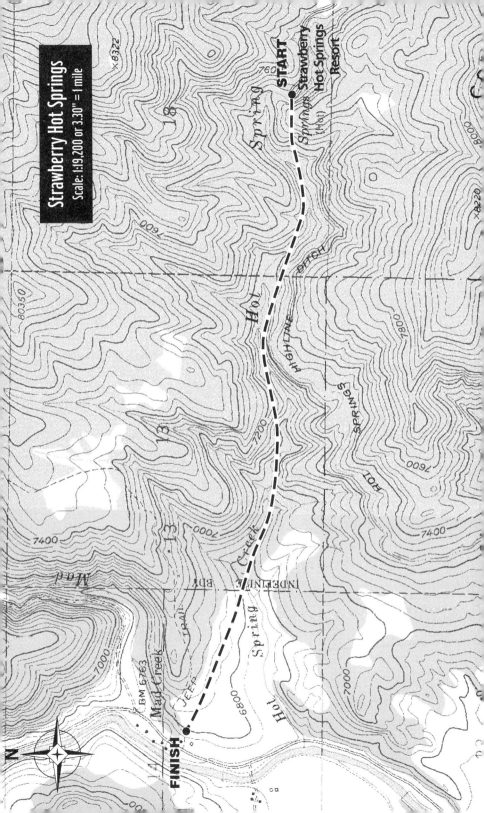

The trail is narrow, and steep-walled canyon rocks will guide you and keep you on the course. The trail can range from light to heavy snow so be prepared to do a little trail packing if you are the first one in after a good snowfall. Otherwise, the trail receives light use and is easy to follow. The view up and down the canyon is serene, picturesque, and uncrowded. A large herd of Rocky Mountain elk winter here and pass through the area on a regular basis—keep your cameras handy and loaded with film.

The trail climbs moderately back out of the canyon and ends at the Mad Creek Village near County Road 129, where there are a group of residential homes. No services are available here. And unfortunately the pull-outs and parking area here along County Road 129 are not plowed on a regular basis.

You can traverse back to the hot springs on the same trail, and the last 0.25 mile is a steep, invigorating climb. Skiers and shoers will find that a good set of ski poles will make climbing out a lot easier!

After returning to the trailhead, grab your swim suit and head to the primitive hot spring pools. Water temperature coming out of the mountain is a scalding 147 degrees Fahrenheit that is "cooled down" to about 104 degrees. The Strawberry Park Hot Springs is open to the public daily from 10 A.M. to 11 P.M. Unlike other hot springs that have built commercial "tubs," here you'll find modified primitive natural pools. Cost per person is less than $10, and towels can be rented for $1.00. Bring your own snacks and drinks.

Directions at a glance

- The trailhead begins at the Strawberry Park Hot Springs parking lot and goes about 200 yards before dropping down to Hot Springs Creek. First 0.25 mile is steep downhill.

- Trail goes west and levels out at the bottom of Hot Springs Creek and continues for approximately 2.5 miles, ending at houses near Mad Creek Village.

- Follow the same trail back to trailhead and the Hot Springs Resort.

How to get there

From Steamboat Springs the Strawberry Park Hot Springs Resort area is approximately 7 miles north of town. Take 7th Avenue north until it turns into County Road 36. County Road 36 will then turn into Forest Route (FR) 323 and dead ends at the Strawberry Park Hot Springs Resort parking lot. Signs will direct you to the Hot Springs Resort. The last 2 miles to the springs are winter rated as "four-wheel-drive only" because the road is steep, icy, and narrow. Limited accessibility is why this area provides plenty of uncrowded skiing/shoeing.

Parking area at the Strawberry Park Hot Springs is small, but for day-use skiers and snowshoers, there are usually a couple of spaces. Hot springs are most popular with the locals and visitors in the afternoon and in the evening, and that's when the parking area gets crowded.

Photo by Tom Stillo, courtesy of Crested Butte Mountain Resort

Rabbit Ears Peak

Steamboat Springs, CO

Type of trail:	▬▬▬➤ ⬭
Also used by:	Snowmobilers
Distance:	5.0 miles
Terrain:	Gentle but constant climb to the top of the Peak and gentle glide/trek back to trailhead.
Trail difficulty:	Intermediate
Surface quality:	Ungroomed but usually tracked by skiers/shoers.
Elevation:	Trailhead 9,600 feet, climbs to 10,651 feet
Time:	3 hours
Avalanche danger:	Low to moderate
Snowmobile use:	Moderate to high
Food and facilities:	Winter services in the area are sparse at best. Fuel up your vehicle, check your equipment, and purchase your drinks, sack lunches, and supplies before leaving Steamboat Springs. The city of Steamboat Springs has great restaurants, grocery/ liquor stores, ski/snowshoe shops and rentals, as well as plenty of motels and bed-and-breakfast accommodations. Call for information about Steamboat Springs and adventures in the area (970–879–0880) or use the Web site: www.steamboat-chamber.com.

Throughout the winter months, the snow is plentiful in this region and allows the outdoor enthusiast excellent opportunities to ski or snowshoe from early to late in the season. If cross-country ski touring is your passion, the gently rolling terrain and open meadows are ideal. Most of the terrain is rated at an intermediate skill level.

The Rabbit Ears Peak is visible from the road and for most of your tour. Called Rabbit Ears Peak because that's exactly what it looks like, the summit is located at an elevation of 10,651 feet. The tour takes you up on the FR 291 road. The route generally follows the main ridgeline of the Continental Divide and traces of old 4 x 4 trails. You'll find stunning volcanic rock formations that were formed millions of years ago when this area was geologically active throughout the area. They make for great photo opportunities.

Once you start the tour, you'll go northwest across a meadow for about 0.5 mile and then enter into a wooded area where there are large stands of pine, spruce, and aspen trees. After entering the forested area,

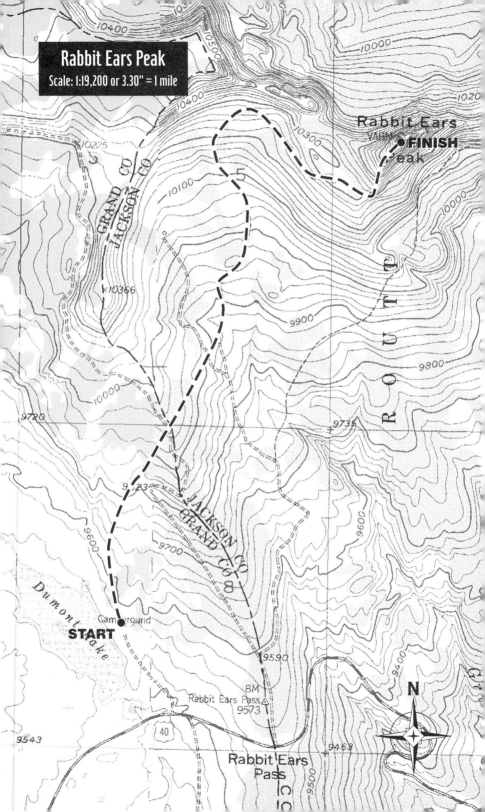

you will see plenty of smaller trails jutting off from the old 4WD road. Most of these trails simply drop off or climb away from the main road and then loop back within 0.25 mile. Be advised that snowmobilers also enjoy this part of the trail, so you may encounter some traffic and noise.

Forest Route (FR) 291 continues a gradual ascent through small meadows and valleys, until ending at the base of the "ears." Several small trails will lead you to the summit, but the Forest Service asks that everyone avoid the temptation to climb the "ears" themselves. The rock is crumbly, very weathered, and is rated unsafe for any climbing.

From the base of the "ears,"

Directions at a glance

- From the trailhead the route follows FR 291 with numerous small cutoffs and old 4 x 4 roads.

- Follow main trail to the base of Rabbit Ears Monument.

- Return to the trailhead using the same trails.

the view at the Continental Divide is spectacular and stretches many miles in several different directions to include much of the Routt National Forest. Mount Zirkel lies to the north, Mount Rawah to the east, and Flat Tops is to the south.

How to get there

The Rabbit Ears Peak area is about 20 miles east of Steamboat Springs. From town take Highway 40 south and then east about 18 miles to the Lake Dumont turnoff. The road will be on your left and is marked with large signs. Follow the main road for approximately 2 miles—past the campground and picnic area—and then turn left at the Rabbit Ears Monument. This will be marked as Forest Road (FR) 311. Go approximately 0.25 mile to where Forest Road (FR) 291 forks off to the right. It's suggested that you park in this area and begin skiing/snowshoeing from this point. FR 291 is where the trail begins, and even though this road may be passable with four-wheel-drive in the late season, it can be slippery and icy.

Brainard Lake

Brainard Lake Recreation Area, Ward, CO

Type of trail:	▬▬▬ ⊙
Distance:	5.0 miles
Terrain:	Rolling hills with gentle climbs and descents.
Trail difficulty:	Easy
Surface quality:	Ungroomed but usually tracked by skiers/shoers.
Elevation:	Trail starts at 10,080 feet and the lake is at 10,345 feet.
Time:	3 hours
Avalanche danger:	Low
Food and facilities:	Located less than 35 miles from downtown Boulder, the Brainard Lake and Cabin Trail is an ideal day-trip location. If you're planning on making the Brainard Cabin your overnight destination, advance reservations are a must! You must also be a member of the Colorado Mountain Club. It's easy to join and costs you a $25 initiation fee and then about $40 per year to retain your membership. At least one member of your ski/snowshoe party must be a member in order to reserve the cabin, which then rents for as little as $10 per night, per person. For information about joining the Colorado Mountain Club, call (303) 554–7688.

Whether you're planning on staying overnight in the Brainard Lake Cabin or just planning a day trip, you'll find that most of the grocery stores, convenience stores, gas stations, restaurants, and overnight accommodations are found in Boulder. Contact the Boulder Chamber of Commerce at (303) 442–1044 for brochures and additional information.

In Nederland, only 4.5 miles to the south, you will find a couple of small restaurants/cafes and a newly built twenty-four-room log hotel called the Lodge at Nederland (800–279–9463). Nederland is also a good roadside stop for last minute snacks, a cup of coffee, or lunch

Often described as the most popular area for cross-country skiing and snowshoeing in all of the Front Range, the Brainard Lake area has two trails—a north and south trail—that will lead skiers/shoers to the actual lake, and a host of small "spur" roads in and around the lake that intersect with a myriad of other wonderful trails that are fun for day

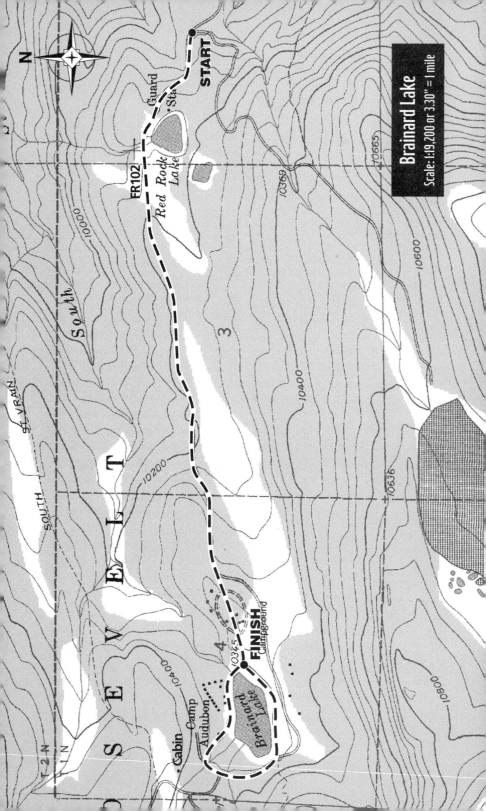

Brainard Lake
Scale: 1:19,200 or 3.30" = 1 mile

use or overnight adventures. To the west the 73,391-acre Indian Peaks Wilderness Area offers unlimited access to valleys carved by ancient glaciers and bowls that tempt the telemark skier and snowshoer who brought along his or her snowboard.

The North Brainard Lake Trail, paralleling or trekking along the often unsheltered summer road, is ideal for beginners who want the experience of backcountry skiing/shoeing along rolling hills and through thick glades of trees with plenty of gentle climbs and descents. Heavily used, it is almost always tracked and easy to follow. Plus it has the added incentive of a cabin at the west end of Brainard Lake.

The Brainard Lake Cabin was built in 1928 and is owned and operated today by the Boulder chapter of the Colorado Mountain Club. The two-story cabin, heated by a fireplace and a wood-burning cookstove, can accommodate up to ten people. As is usual with all backcountry cabins and huts, the water is obtained by melting snow. To use this hut at least one member of your group must be an active member of the Colorado Mountain Club.

From the snow closure gate, head north and west from the Red Rock Lake trailhead for 0.25 mile, ascending gradually and bending around a ridge. The trail contours to the west above South St. Vrain Creek and flattens out, paralleling the main road. At a little more than 0.5 mile from the trailhead, you'll cross a small creek that flows north from the Red Rock Lake into St. Vrain Creek. Continue west along the road or take one of the many other trails that also runs west and parallels the road.

At about 2.0 miles, you'll see several small cabins and huts along the road. Continue to trek/ski west toward Brainard Lake. At the edge of Brainard Lake, the trail forks. It's actually a loop around the lake. If the

Directions at a glance

- Trailhead begins at the parking area at the end of FR 102.

- Take the trail west from the parking lot along the road to Red Rock Lake or take any one of the many trails that head west.

- At approximately 2.0 miles from the trailhead, you'll see several cabins and huts. Continue to trek/ski west to the edge of Brainard Lake.

- At Brainard Lake, the rail forks. Take the trail to the right, north and west around the north shore of the lake if the cabin is your destination. You'll see plenty of signs.

- Or if you want to loop around Brainard Lake, take either of the trails.

- To return to the trailhead, follow the same route you came in on back to the parking lot or enjoy many of the parallel trails.

Brainard Cabin is your goal, ski or snowshoe along the trail to the right, heading north and west. You'll see the signs pointing out the way to the cabin on the north shore of the lake, less than 0.5 mile from the fork in the trail.

To return to the parking lot you have a few choices. You can go back the way you came along the summer Brainard Lake Road to the south, which circles the lake and then heads east. Or you can take the North Trail, which is a little longer and a little more challenging. Skirting along the south side of the lake, the South Trail is usually tracked and easy to follow and is a pristine route through the trees.

If you're not quite ready to return and want to explore more of the area, there are a myriad of other routes intertwined with the trails to Brainard Lake. Mitchell Lake is well suited to intermediate skiers, Blue Lake is more for the advanced skier, and Long Lake is for the novice.

How to get there

From Boulder go west approximately 17 miles on Route 119 to Nederland. Once you've driven into the middle of the town make a right on Colorado Route 72 and go north approximately 15 miles on to the town of Ward. Just north of Ward take the turnoff and go left on the road to the Brainard Lake Recreation Area. It's well signed and marked as Forest Road (FR) 102. Drive on this paved road west for 2.5 miles to where the road is closed for the winter and blocked by a gate. You'll see an area to park at the snow closure fence area.

Photo by Tari and Andy Lightbody

Middle St. Vrain

Allens Park/Peaceful Valley, CO

Type of trail:	▬▬▬ 🔵
Also used by:	Snowmobilers
Distance:	10.0 miles
Terrain:	Gentle but constant climb up the trail. Plenty of areas to jump off for downhill glides and treks.
Trail difficulty:	Novice/intermediate
Surface quality:	Ungroomed but usually tracked by skiers/shoers.
Elevation:	Trail starts at 8,600 feet and ends at 11,533 feet at Lake Gibraltar.
Time:	Full day
Avalanche danger:	Low to moderate
Snowmobile use:	There is snowmobile traffic in the Middle St. Vrain Valley until you cross into the Indian Peaks Wilderness Area at 4.8 miles from the trailhead.
Food and facilities:	The Middle St. Vrain Trail has few if any close-by facilities. Located about 35 miles from Longmont and Boulder, most of the grocery stores, convenience stores, gas stations, restaurants, and overnight accommodations are going to be found there. It's best to plan on making advance overnight accommodations in either of these two cities. Contact the Boulder Chamber of Commerce at (303) 442–1044 for brochures and additional information.

In this neck of the woods, trails abound everywhere and virtually parallel each other and intersect at various places along their routes. At almost any point you can jump off one trail and ski/shoe or snowboard through the fresh, deep powder snow, then travel a short distance and catch up with another trail. The Middle St. Vrain Road is the main route that heads west over the valley floor of Middle St. Vrain Creek, entering deep into the alpine forests and the Indian Peaks Wilderness. The road ends farther ahead, and the St. Vrain Glacier Trail begins—stretching several miles into the wilderness. The trail ends at the high-meadow Gibraltar Lake, where you'll stare, wide-eyed, at the magnificent swirling ice sculptures of the St. Vrain Glaciers.

The route along the Middle St. Vrain Trail follows a 4x4 road and is relatively flat and easy. Technically only novice skills are necessary for skiers and shoers. The difficulty comes later in the trail when you get

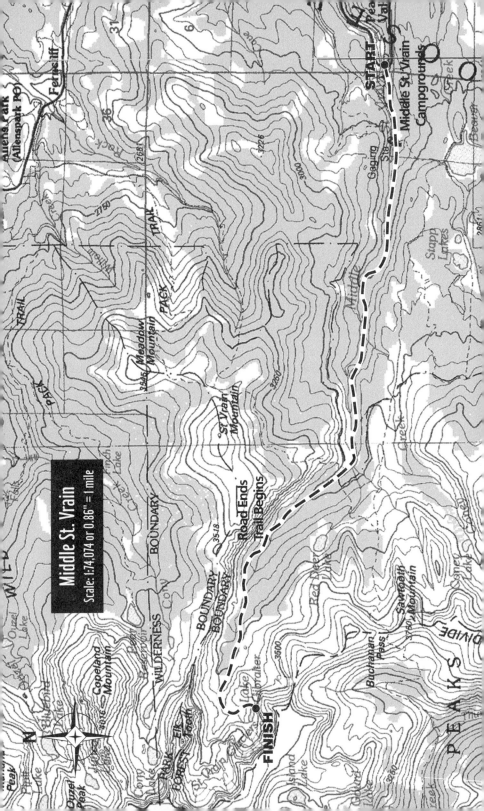

Middle St. Vrain

Scale: 1:74,074 or 0.86" = 1 mile

above treeline and encounter not only harsher weather conditions, but a trail of considerable distance that is remote and not heavily used. For days after a fresh powdery snow, if you are going to access the area, you had better plan on being able to do the trail breaking.

Part of the beauty of the Middle St. Vrain Creek Trail is that you can turn back along the route whenever you want and glide/trek gently back down to the trailhead. But for those who venture all the way to the end of the trail, the remote valley, the ice cirques of the glaciers, and Elk Tooth Mountain at 12,848 feet make the inspiring trip more than worth the effort.

From the parking area, head west through the Middle St. Vrain Campground and across the creek. For the first mile, the 4x4-vehicle road contours southwest into and out of the trees, climbing gradually. The

Directions at a glance

- Park at the end of the plowed area west of Highway 72.
- Head west from the parking area to the trailhead. Go west and follow the 4x4 road climbing gently for the first 3.0 miles.
- At just under 5.0 miles from the trailhead, look for signs indicating that you are entering the Indian Peaks Wilderness Area.
- About 0.25 mile into the Wilderness Area, you'll climb a relatively steep 14 percent grade, cross a stream, and intersect a trail at the northern end of the meadow.
- Head northwest over the next 2.0 miles of level terrain to the southwest corner of St. Vrain Mountain.
- At approximately 7.5 miles from the trailhead, the route will fork. Take the right fork heading north and west.
- Road ends at just under 8.0 miles from the trailhead, and the well-signed St. Vrain Glacier Trail begins.
- If a novice skier/shoer, you may want to turn around at this point. If not, plan on breaking your own trail as you continue west along the creek.
- At about 9.5 miles from the trailhead, you'll ascend the open slopes to see Lake Gibraltar and the Elk Tooth Mountain.
- Contour around Lake Gibraltar and enjoy the magnificent views of Elk Tooth Mountain as well as the St. Vrain Glaciers.
- Return to the trailhead using the same route you used to come into the area.

next 2.0 miles will take you deep within the scattered trees, sheltered from the wind, meandering to the north before veering, again, to the west. The road continues much the same way, paralleling the St. Vrain Creek into the forests of the Roosevelt National Forest.

At a little under 5.0 miles from the trailhead, you'll enter the Indian Peaks Wilderness Area. Here no form of mechanized travel is permitted. Alone with the trees and snow as your audience, you'll encounter one relatively steep hill with a 14 percent grade, cross a stream, and intersect another trail at the northern end of a meadow. Entering back into the woods, you'll head sharply northwest over more level terrain for the next 2.0 miles, skiing/shoeing along the southwest corner of St. Vrain Mountain. On the north side of the valley the slopes become noticeably more rugged and craggy. At about 7.5 miles in, there'll be a fork in the 4x4 road. Take the right fork, heading more north and west.

A little farther ahead the road ends and turns into St. Vrain Glacier Trail. It's well marked and is a good turnaround point if you are a beginner skier/shoer who doesn't want to continue on and have to break trail. If you feel adventurous, however, continue to follow the creek west, climb over two steep hills that are back to back. At about the 9.5-mile point, you'll break out of the trees and ascend up the open slopes, looking out over the incredible vistas of Elk Tooth Mountain.

The trail now bends around to the southwest and climbs up the last set of steep slopes to Lake Gibraltar at 11,332 feet. Before you, at the head of the valley, are the indescribable St. Vrain Glaciers, stretching to the Continental Divide.

After some breathtaking views and some great photo opportunities, you follow the same route for the return trip to the road and trailhead. As you might imagine, it's somewhat quicker because you can follow your tracks and ski slightly downhill all the way back to your car.

How to get there

From Denver take Highway 287 north to the north edge of Longmont. It's about 37.0 miles from downtown Denver. Make a left and head west on the classic Route 66. Go about 8 miles until Route 66 turns into U.S. Highway 36, continuing west. Follow U.S. Highway 36 another 1.75 miles through the small town of Lyons. Turn left, heading south on Route 7. Go approximately 14.75 miles to the junction of Highway 72. Make a left on Highway 72, go about 4.0 miles, and you'll end up in Peaceful Valley. At the west side of Peaceful Valley, Highway 72 curves south and then heads east. At the far western end look for the signs to the St. Vrain Campground. Park in a plowed area west of Highway 72.

Lost Lake
Nederland, CO

Type of trail:	▬▬▬ ⬤
Also used by:	Snowmobilers
Distance:	6.0 miles
Terrain:	Gentle climbs and descents with lots of open areas.
Trail difficulty:	Novice/intermediate
Surface quality:	Ungroomed but usually well tracked by skiers/shoers.
Elevation:	Trail starts at 8,810 feet and ends at Lost Lake, elevation 9,780 feet.
Time:	3 to 4 hours
Avalanche danger:	Low
Snowmobile use:	Moderate
Food and facilities:	Located less than 30 miles from downtown Boulder, the Eldora Ski Resort and the Lost Lake Trail are ideal day-trip locations. You'll find grocery stores, convenience stores, gas stations, restaurants, and overnight accommodations in Boulder. Contact the Boulder Chamber of Commerce at (303) 442–1044 for brochures and additional information.

In Nederland, you will find a couple of small restaurants/cafes and a newly built twenty-four-room log hotel called the Lodge at Nederland (800–279–9463). Nederland also has a couple of small independent motels and bed-and-breakfast facilities. It's also good roadside stop for last minute snacks, a cup of coffee, or lunch.

The Eldora Ski Resort is located just minutes from the Lost Lake trailhead. At the resort there's a full cafeteria and cocktail lounge. There are no overnight facilities at the resort so plan accordingly. They do have a full line of cross-country ski and snowshoe rentals however. Call (303) 440–8700 for additional information.

Popular because of its proximity to the heavily populated cities of Denver and Boulder, this area is laced with trails. The tour to Lost Lake is a fun outing for any level skier or snowshoer who wants to enjoy the beauty of a high-elevation mountain lake. Well tracked, not too long, and with manageable elevation gains, this tour is ideal for beginners who want to discover the sport of cross-country skiing, or for snowshoers who want to take a pleasant walk without losing their breath. Only a cou-

Lost Lake

Scale: 1:16,000 or 3.96" = 1 mile

START

FINISH

Lost Lake

Hessie

Fork

TRAIL

Cr.

Minera

Road

N

ple sections of the trail, especially the last one that actually leads to the lake, offer fairly steep hills. Snowshoers will think it's a breeze.

From the unplowed road at the parking area, ski or snowshoe west. The road winds, alternating between sections heading northwest and then dipping to the south and then veering northwest again. At the 1.0-mile point, you'll see a fork in the road going north. Choose the fork to the left, or west. It is well marked with a sign for Hessie Road. Continue on to descend into the valley of the South Fork of Boulder Stream. Soon you'll come to the old townsite of Hessie. The entire Eldora area at the base of Ute Mountain was once a hard rock mining community. Remnants of old gold and silver mines dot the backcountry all throughout the area.

Continue west past Hessie, cross over the North Fork of Middle Boulder Creek, and then maneuver over a series of sharp turns that switchback up a moderately steep hill. Beginners will be happy that the trail flattens out at about the 2.0-mile point. Traversing a vehicle bridge, you'll cross over the South Fork of Middle Boulder Creek, climb moderately through a clearing, and see the trail marker to Lost Lake at a little over the 2.5-mile point.

Head south, careful not to choose the trail to King Lake, which heads off almost directly west. The final portion of the Lost Lake trail is only 0.5 mile in length and will climb up a hillside through the trees. You'll pass another fork—again, go south. The trail will then bend to the west through a meadow before contouring east and ascending to the lake.

From the lake you should be able to see an abandoned mine on the craggy slopes of Bryan Mountain to the south. To the north you can view

Directions at a glance

- Parking and trailhead will be at end of Road 130 where the snow closure is located.

- Take the trail west along the road for approximately 1.0 mile.

- Trail will fork at the 1.0-mile point. Take the fork to the left, heading west. Watch for signs indicating Hessie Road.

- Descend into the valley along the South Fork of Boulder Stream and ski/shoe the townsite of Hessie.

- Continue west past Hessie, crossing over the North Fork of Middle Boulder Creek.

- Trail climbs and then flattens out at about 2.0 miles from the trailhead.

- Traverse a vehicle bridge and cross over the South Fork of Middle Boulder Creek.

- Watch for trail marker to Lost Lake at about the 2.5-mile point.

- Avoid trails that go west. Continue south about 0.5 mile to the edge of Lost Lake.

- Return to the trailhead using the same route you came in on.

Chittenden Mountain. Lost Lake is a great spot to sit, relax, enjoy lunch, and take in the beauty of the Rocky Mountains. When you're ready to return home for the day, simply follow the same route you came in on back to the trailhead.

How to get there
From Boulder go west approximately 17 miles on Route 119 to the town of Nederland. Go through the town and watch for signs to the Eldora Ski Resort. Make a right on Road 130 and go approximately 4 miles to the Eldora Ski Resort. A little ways past Eldora, the road will not be plowed and snow will block further travel. Park alongside the road.

Jenny Lind Gulch
Nederland, CO

Type of trail:	▬▬ ◁▷
Also used by:	Snowmobilers
Distance:	5.0 miles
Terrain:	Gentle ascents and large open bowls
Trail difficulty:	Novice to intermediate
Surface quality:	Ungroomed but usually well tracked by skiers/shoers.
Elevation:	Trail begins at 8,800 feet and ends at the springs—elevation 9,850 feet.
Time:	3 to 5 hours
Avalanche danger:	Low along the trail, moderate in the open bowls
Snowmobile use:	Low to moderate
Food and facilities:	Located less than 30 miles from downtown Boulder, the Jenny Lind Gulch Trail is an ideal day-trip location. You'll find grocery stores, convenience stores, gas stations, restaurants, and overnight accommodations in Boulder. Contact the Boulder Chamber of Commerce at (303) 442–1044 for brochures and additional information.

In Nederland you will find a couple of small restaurants and cafes and a newly built twenty-four-room log hotel called the Lodge at Nederland (800–279–9463). Nederland is also a good roadside stop for last minute snacks on the way in, or a cup of coffee, or lunch on the way out of the area. There are no facilities once you start out on the Jenny Lind Gulch Trail.

A short trail convenient for those working and living close to Denver, this route has it all in midwinter—a beginning section ideal for the novice skier/snowshoer and then 600-foot bowls at the upper end where intermediate and advanced skiers, shoers, and even snowboarders can practice carving their turns. Located in an open meadow, the beginning part of the trail is sometimes windy, but you'll soon enter the trees, and the trail is sheltered. Weekdays are the best time to use the Jenny Lind Gulch Trail and area because of weekend crowding.

From the trailhead ski or snowshoe south on the four-wheel-drive vehicle trail. The trail forks at about an eighth of a mile from the trailhead, and you need to take the right branch into and out of a stand of trees. At a little over 0.5 mile, you'll pass one of three creeks that drain into the Jenny Lind Gulch from the west. Cross to the west side of the creek and keep your eyes open for the remnants of old mines on Dakota Hill to the east. These remnants are from the old Melrose Mine, a gold and silver operation that dates back to the early 1900s.

At about the 1.0-mile point the trail gets steeper, heading west over a wooded valley. Grades are anywhere from 18 percent to about 26 percent. After another 1.0 mile, you'll bend around to the southwest, and the trail pops out of the trees, ending at the Springs. Intermediate and advanced skiers, boarders, and shoers will want to continue on to the top of the bowl, climbing 650 feet to the 10,470-foot ridge-line. For skiers the area is ideal for practicing their telemark turns on the way down. If you shoed in and brought your snowboard, the big bowls are a great way to get back down off the mountain in a hurry!

If you are a novice skier or snowshoer and don't feel you want a hefty climb, head back the way you came.

Directions at a glance

- Look for the closed gate on south side of Road 16.

- Ski/shoe south on four-wheel-drive trail. At an eighth of a mile from trailhead, the route forks. Take the right fork.

- At 0.5 mile, you'll cross the creek to the west side of Jenny Lind Gulch.

- Look for the remnants of the old Melrose Mine to the east on Dakota Hill.

- At about 1.0 mile from the trailhead, the route gets steeper and climbs steadily for the next 2.0 miles.

- Trail ends at the Springs and where the open bowls are ideal for skiing or boarding downhill.

How to get there

From Boulder go west approximately 17 miles on Route 119 to the town of Nederland. Go through the town and continue on Route 119 south for another 5 miles to the small town of Rollinsville. Make a left and go west on Road 16—marked as the road to the East Portal. Continue west approximately 5 miles and look for trail sign to Jenny Lind Gulch. It is approximately 1 mile before you get to the even smaller town of Tolland. The closed gate on the south side of the road is the trailhead. Park along side Road 16.

Photo by Mark Fox, courtesy of Copper Mountain Resort

Second Creek Cabin/Winter Park Ski Resort

Berthoud Pass, Winter Park, CO

Type of trail: ▬▬ ◉

Also used by: Downhill skiers at the Winter Park Ski Resort

Distance: 3.0 miles to and from Second Creek Hut; 5.5 miles from trailhead to Winter Park Ski Resort (shuttle required for return trip)

Terrain: Gentle ascents and open areas for first 2 miles, and then more challenging climbs and descents to end of trail at the Ski Resort.

Trail difficulty: Novice to intermediate

Surface quality: Ungroomed but usually well tracked by skiers/shoers for first 2 miles. Then ungroomed backcountry conditions for rest of trail.

Elevation: Trail starts at 10,580 feet. Second Creek Hut is at 11,200 feet, and the Winter Park Ski Resort base is at 9,360 feet.

Time: 3 to 4 hours to the Hut and back.

5 hours to all day from trailhead to Ski Resort.

Avalanche danger: Low to moderate on the trail to Second Creek Hut. There can be high avalanche danger in the bowls on the sides of the valleys.

Food and facilities: Located less than two hours from downtown Denver, a lot of people come up to Berthoud Pass for day use only. Coming out of Denver, there are a lot of small towns located along I–70 with small convenience stores, gas stations, and restaurants.

If you're planning on staying over, the closest full-service restaurants and overnight accommodations are found at the Winter Park Ski Resort. From the Second Creek Camp ground and trailhead, they're located a short 6.5 miles north on Highway 40. For information about hotels, motels, condos, and their facilities, call (970) 726–5514. The Winter Park Ski Resort also has a cross-country and snowshoe rental/repair shop, as well as access to a lot of skier/shoer trails and ranches throughout the area.

For information about the Second Creek Hut/Gwen Andrews Hut, contact the U.S. Forest Service at (970) 887–4100. (Forest Service representatives say they are hopeful that the cabin will be re-opened for day use and overnight guests by the 1998–99 winter season.)

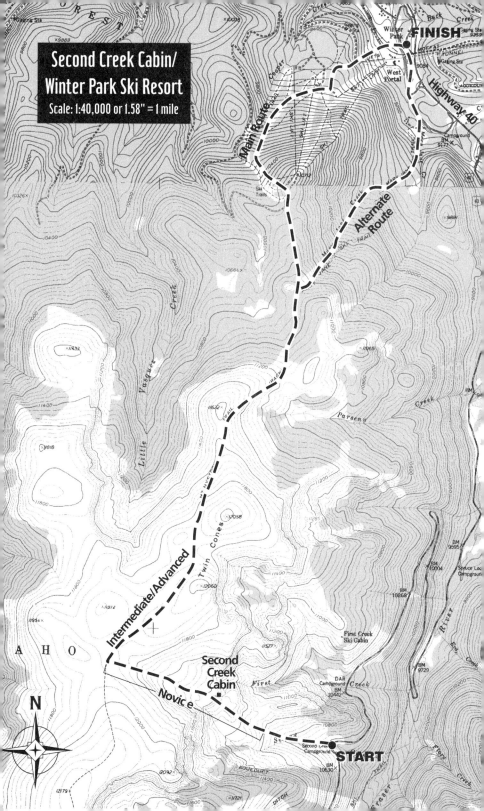

The Berthoud Pass area is one of the most popular areas in the state for all types of winter sports for many excellent reasons. It's close to the Denver area and so is convenient to get to. Skiers/snowshoers can combine backcountry adventures with a little downhill at the close-by Winter Park Ski Resort or the newly reopened Berthoud Pass Ski Area for which the snow is usually excellent. Plus there are all sorts of terrains available for cross-country touring, telemark skiing, and snowshoeing.

The tour to the Second Creek Hut is short and scenic. Unfortunately the First Creek Cabin and the Second Creek Hut have fallen into disrepair in recent years, and the U.S. Forest Service has taken control back from a local ski group that was managing the facilities. At present the Second Creek Hut, also known as the Gwen Andrews Hut, is closed to the public, but planners at the Forest Service say that they are confident that they can refurbish the cabins and hopefully have one or more open for the 1998–99 winter season.

From the trailhead ski on the west side of the road, over the valley, staying on the north or on the right side of the creek. You'll start to climb through the trees; the path is generally well marked. Be sure to stay clear of the slopes on the south side of the valley because extreme avalanche dangers may exist. Keep heading west and you'll discover the trees thin out as you climb higher.

At about midway through the trail, you'll reach the steepest section on an open slope. Stay to the north as you climb and then, when the terrain flattens a bit, bend around to the south edge of the ridgeline.

You'll traverse a valley and follow the trail over another ridge, ascending north. At the top of the ridge, veer to the west and to the A-frame hut nestled by the trees. It's close to where Second Creek starts and breaks away to the south from First Creek.

If you want to extend your tour to the First Creek Valley, head northwest for a little over 1.0 mile and connect with the Mount Nystrom Trail. Veer northeast and follow the trail leading to the top of the main north-south ridge above the First Creek valley. Be careful of avalanche chutes on the southern side of the drainage. The trail starts out to the north and is pretty flat for the first 1.0 mile. After that it drops with grades upward of 38 percent and will lead you all the way to the Winter Park Ski Resort. If you decide to take the entire route, at about 3.0 miles down the Mount Nystrom Trail, the route will fork. The path to the right leads you down the Mary Jane Ski Trail along Mary Jane Creek. It's about 1.75 miles down through some pretty steep (40 to 50 percent) drops to the main road, which will lead you to the base of the Winter Park Ski Resort.

The trail that goes to the left has another 300-foot climb to the north;

Directions at a glance

- The trailhead begins at the parking area. Ski/shoe west over the valley, stay on the north or right side of the creek. First 0.75 mile is relatively flat with gentle climbs. Stay clear of slopes on south side because avalanche dangers may exist.

- At 0.75-mile mark, the trail steepens for an eighth mile as you traverse around the hill.

- At the 1.0-mile point, the trail flattens out and crosses the valley to your west and north.

- Look for the Second Creek Hut across the valley.

- Return to the trailhead by the same route.

Alternate route

- From the Second Creek Campground, take a shuttle vehicle and drive 6.5 miles north on Highway 40 to the Winter Park Ski Resort.

- Return to the Second Creek Campground and follow route to the Second Creek Hut.

- Instead of turning around, intermediate/advanced skiers will traverse open area in a northwest direction from the hut and intersect with the Mount Nystrom Trail.

- Turn right, heading north on the Mount Nystrom Trail. Be cautious of avalanche chutes in the area.

- Mount Nystrom Trail is on relatively flat terrain for first 1.0 mile.

- The next 2.0 miles of the trail are steep up- and downhill grades designed for advanced skiers/shoers.

- At just over 3 miles along the Mount Nystrom Trail, the route forks.

- Trail to the right takes you down steep switchbacks along the Mary Jane Ski Trail for about 1.75 miles to the base area of the Winter Park Ski Resort.

- Trail to the left climbs steeply for a short distance and then descends down to the top of the ski lifts at the Winter Park Ski Resort.

- Both trails will take you to the base area at the Winter Park Ski Resort.

- Pick up shuttle car and return to the trailhead at Second Creek Campground.

then it drops down to the top of the Winter Park Ski area. It's a little gentler descent, but keep in mind that for the last 1.0 mile of downhill, you'll be on the ski slope with faster-moving downhill skiers.

With both trails ending up at the Winter Park Ski Resort, it's a great place to relax and get something warm to drink and eat before picking up your shuttle car to shag the vehicle you left at the Second Creek trailhead.

How to get there

From Denver, head west on I–70 for approximately 42.0 miles to U.S. Highway 40. Take Highway 40 west/north approximately 15.5 miles to the top of Berthoud Pass—located between Empire and Winter Park. Three miles past the summit of Berthoud Pass look for the turnout to the Second Creek Campground. Parking can be found on the west side of the road. If you're planning on skiing/shoeing all the way to the Winter Park Ski Resort area, you'll need to take your shuttle vehicle another 6.5 miles north on Highway 40 and park it in the lot at the ski resort.

Mount Bierstadt

Guanella Pass, Georgetown, CO

Type of trail:	▬▬ 🟫
Also used by:	Snowmobilers
Distance:	6.2 miles
Terrain:	Steep and challenging climbs all the way to the summit.
Trail difficulty:	Advanced/expert
Surface quality:	Ungroomed and usually not well tracked by skiers/shoers.
Elevation:	Trail starts at 11,650 feet and ends at the summit at 14,060 feet.
Time:	5 to 7 hours
Avalanche danger:	Low to high, depending on conditions
Snowmobile use:	Moderate traffic exists in flats of Guanella Valley.
Food and facilities:	In and around the Guanella Pass area, there is little in the way of food or facilities. Closest moderate-size town is Georgetown, 11 miles back north on the Guanella Pass Road. Hotels, motels, restaurants, grocery stores, and gas stations can be found in the Georgetown area. Contact the Georgetown Chamber of Commerce at (303) 569–2888 for information about facilities in the area.

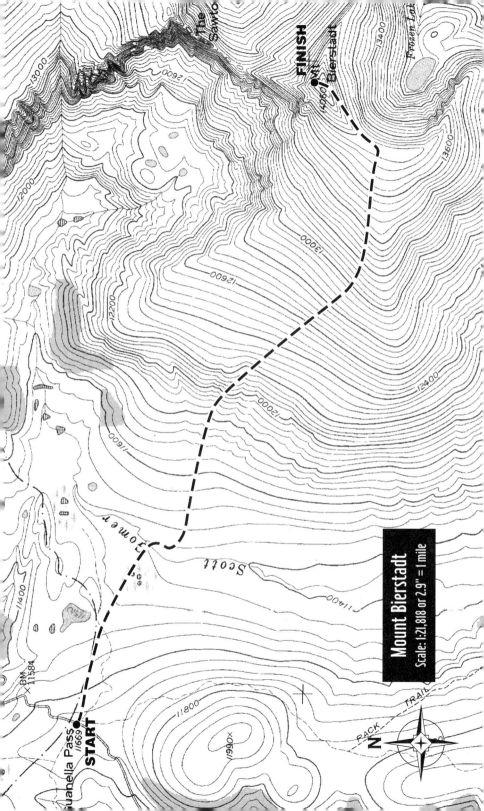

f you want the experience of snowshoeing or cross-country skiing up one of Colorado's "Fourteeners," the Guanella Pass route to Mount Bierstadt is one of the best. The route is steep in sections, and the trail difficult to follow and exposed without the shelter of trees. But if the hardships don't scare you away, the view from the summit of one of the highest mountains in the state—overlooking metropolitan Denver to the east and Breckenridge, Keystone, and Vail to the west—will make you think you can see forever!

During the summer months all the many trails from Guanella Pass are loaded with hikers. During the winter the crowds clear out, and the route attracts snow climbers, skiers, snowshoers, and mountaineers. Be sure to check the avalanche conditions and only make this tour when the potential for slides is rated as low. Just keep remembering and reminding yourself as you ascend the 2,400-foot grade in just over 3.0 miles that for the mountain climbers this tour is rated one of the easiest for a "Fourteener." For cross-country skiers, think of the downhill ride on the way back!

From the trailhead and parking area, ski or snowshoe southeast along what is called "Guanella Flats" about 0.75 mile to Scott Gomer Creek. Enjoy the descending grade on this short stretch because after you cross the creek, it'll be uphill all the way to the summit. After crossing Scott Gomer Creek, aim and angle your journey toward the headwall to the southeast.

Directions at a glance

- The trailhead at Guanella Pass begins at the parking area.

- Follow trail southeast through the Guanella Flats approximately 0.75-mile and cross Scott Gomer Creek.

- Angle/aim toward the "headwall" to the southeast. Begin steep climb up the headwall to the north, ascending 20 percent-plus grades.

- Go another 0.25 mile and then head southeast until reaching the southwest ridgeline.

- Traverse the ridgeline for another 0.50 mile.

- Head north around the peak for the last 0.25 mile to the summit of 14,060-foot Mount Bierstadt.

- Return to the trailhead back down the same route and enjoy steep gliding/trekking.

If you're lucky you'll be able to see tracks and trail from skiers and shoers who have come through the area and broken the trail for you. If not, a good topo map, compass, and a GPS unit along with excellent navigating skills are a must on this advanced skier/shoer trail. At about the 1.0-mile point, you'll need to start veering to the left, ascending the 20 percent-plus grades north up the headwall.

Take a deep breath and tell yourself you're one-third of the way there. Head south–southeast for the next mile or so, ascending over 700 feet until you get to the southwest ridge of the summit. Turn east and keep climbing. After crossing another 0.50 mile of ridgeline and almost 650 feet in additional elevation, you'll veer to the north and contour around the peak for the last 0.25 mile to the Mount Bierstadt summit at 14,060 feet.

Congratulations, you now have a "Fourteener" to put in your ski/shoe logbook of adventures! For people who appreciate the real "Rocky Mountain high," that's a badge of high esteem. On your return down the mountain, the snow from the summit to the southwest ridge may not be the greatest. But from the ridgeline all the way down to the flats—and especially back down the headwall area—you're in for the thrill of your life.

How to get there

Drive west from Denver on I–70 approximately 57 miles to the Georgetown turnoff. Follow the main route through Georgetown to the Guanella Pass Road, located at the southwest edge of town. Turn south on Guanella Pass Road and drive on the winding route for approximately 11 miles, (it'll become a dirt road) to the summit and park at the summit or slightly to the north.

Loveland Pass

Georgetown, CO

Type of trail:	▬▬ ▭
Also used by:	Downhill skiers/snowboarders at Loveland Ski Area resort; some snowmobilers
Distance:	2.5 miles from trailhead to Loveland Ski resort; shuttle vehicle required for return trip
Terrain:	Moderately challenging climbs and great downhill runs to the ski resort.
Trail difficulty:	Intermediate
Surface quality:	Ungroomed but usually well tracked by skiers/shoers.
Elevation:	Trail starts at 11,990 feet and ends at 10,795 at the base of the Loveland Ski Resort.
Time:	5 to 7 hours
Avalanche danger:	Low
Snowmobile use:	Low to moderate
Food and facilities:	The Loveland Pass trail is centrally located between the cities of Georgetown, 12 miles to the east, and the Dillon/Frisco area, 12 miles to the west. Both have plenty of motels, hotels, and bed-and-breakfast facilities. For information about overnight accommodations in the Dillon and Frisco area, call the Summit County Chamber of Commerce at (800) 530–3099. For information about staying in Georgetown or nearby to the Loveland Ski Area resort, call (800) 736–3754 or (800) 225–5683.

Both Georgetown and Dillon/Frisco have plenty of gas stations, markets, convenience stores, etc. With the ski/snowshoe trail ending at the Loveland Ski resort, there are plenty of restaurants, cafeterias, and lounges located at the base area.

The premier stagecoach route built back in 1879, the Loveland Pass area offers magnificent vistas in just about every direction. Mount Sniktau at 12,800 feet rises to the northeast as Clear Creek Valley stretches below. Mounts Trelease and Pettingell lie to the north, while the mighty Saguache and Ten-Mile Range peaks touch the sky to the southwest. Towering above all of them are two "Fourteeners"—the snow-capped Torrey's Peak at 14,261 feet and Mount Bierstadt at 14,060 to the south. If you're into the Rocky Mountain high experience, the Loveland Pass area has views that are unsurpassed.

Understandably, because of such magnificent views and scenery all around, the Loveland Pass is a favorite starting point for a host of winter recreation opportunities. The Loveland Pass cross-country trail that heads to the north is short and boasts a thrilling descent that attracts downhill skiers and even a few snowboarders—almost as much as cross-country skiers and shoers. Be careful, at times it can and will get a bit crowded.

From the trailhead ski or snowshoe west from the summit of Loveland Pass. Follow the trail as it bends around a craggy slope and descends into areas of open bowls. At about the 0.5-mile point, you'll contour around to the north and head downhill on a steep grade that'll take you to the trees below. A little after the 1.0-mile point, you'll intersect with Highway 6. Cross over it and continue skiing/shoeing downhill to the Loveland Ski Area resort.

After crossing the highway, descend along the drainage/creek area that comes from the Eastern Portal. You'll follow the creek for about 1.0 mile. The route will be a little steep at first but will level out and become a more pleasant trail. At about the 2.0-mile point from the trailhead, you'll see the ski area and intersect paths with downhill skiers who are enjoying the groomed trails at the Loveland Ski resort.

Ski or trek down to the Loveland Ski resort base area, and you'll find plenty of places to relax, have lunch, and then either retrieve your shuttle vehicle or seek hotel or motel transportation back to the trailhead to pick up your vehicle.

Directions at a glance

- Follow the trail from the Loveland Pass parking area west for about 0.75 mile.

- Turn north from the open areas and head north. There's lot of open trails, so you can pick the one you like.

- At about 1.0 mile from the trailhead, you'll intersect Highway 6. Cross over the highway.

- Follow the drainage/creek from the East Portal downhill for 1.0 mile.

- At the bottom of the hill, look for the Loveland Ski Area resort area on your left and join the main downhill ski/shoe runs to the base area.

- Pick up your shuttle vehicle and return to Loveland Pass to retrieve your car.

How to get there

From Denver head west on I–70 approximately 56 miles. Take the U.S. Highway 6 turnoff (exit 216), just before the Eisenhower Tunnel. Make a left onto U.S. Highway 6 and go south for about 5 miles to the summit of Loveland Pass. Park in the marked area on the east side of the road. Because you'll be finishing at the Loveland Ski Area resort, you'll need to arrange for some form of transportation to get you back to the summit of the pass. The best advice is to park a shuttle car down at the Loveland Ski Area resort. However, if you're staying at one of the area hotels or motels, chances are excellent that they'll provide complimentary transportation back up to the Loveland Pass area so that you can retrieve your car.

Photo by Roy Kasting ©, courtesy of O₂ Productions, www.westernlight.com

Keystone Gulch

Keystone Ski Resort, Keystone, CO

Type of trail:	▬▬▬ ⬤
Also used by:	Skiers, snowmobilers
Distance:	10.0 miles to and from the bottom of the steep switchbacks; 5.0 miles up the switchbacks to the Top of the Outback Ski lift and back
Terrain:	Moderately challenging climbs for beginners and then steep steps up to the top of the ski resort's lift.
Trail difficulty:	Novice to intermediate
Surface quality:	Ungroomed, but sometimes tracked by skiers/shoers.
Elevation:	Trail starts at about 9,200 feet, ends at 11,960 feet
Time:	5 to 7 hours
Avalanche danger:	Low
Snowmobile use:	Only those belonging to the Keystone Ski Resort are allowed on the trail for maintenance.
Food and facilities:	Located about 5.0 miles from the town of Dillon, the Keystone Gulch Trail is close to facilities in Dillon and the Keystone Ski Resort. Hotels and motels in Dillon provide moderately priced overnight accommodations. There are also grocery stores, convenience stores, gas stations, and a host of restaurants: fast foods to complete sit-down facilities. For brochure information about the facilities in Dillon, contact the Summit County Chamber of Commerce (800) 530–3099.

At the Keystone Ski Resort where the Keystone Gulch Trail begins, you'll find several restaurants, cafeterias, and lounges, including two restaurants rated with four stars by AAA! You have a choice of five different hotels and inns located at the base of the Keystone Ski Resort. Keystone's Nordic Center has a full line of equipment rentals/repairs. They also offer lessons and even moonlight tours. Information on lodging, guides, and tours can be obtained by calling (800) 258–9553.

The Keystone area has over 15.0 kilometers of groomed trails and an additional 35.0 kilometers of backcountry trails in the region. The Keystone Gulch Trail is a fun and popular route because it runs up alongside the southwest boundary of the ski areas and is convenient for

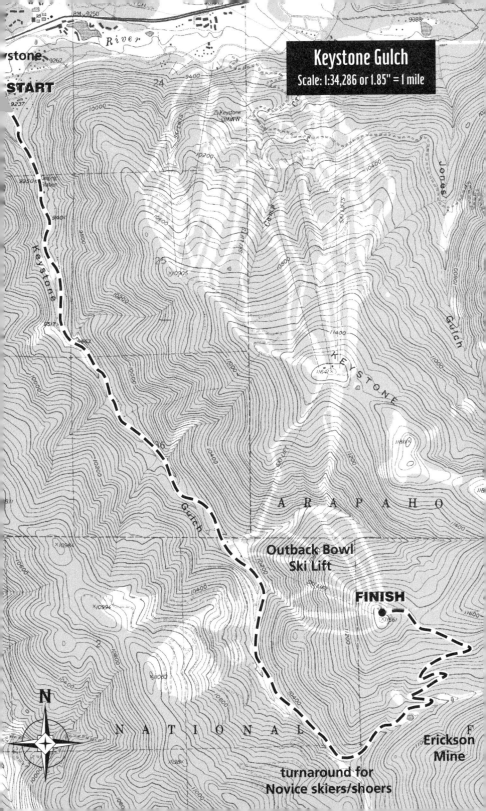

Keystone Gulch
Scale: 1:34,286 or 1.85" = 1 mile

START

FINISH

Outback Bowl
Ski Lift

Erickson
Mine

turnaround for
Novice skiers/shoers

N

downhillers who want to try cross-country touring or snowshoeing for a different adventure. The only snowmobiles you'll ever see belong to employees of the resort who are trekking across their own boundaries and, hopefully, not into yours. The trail presents a gradual climb that only at the end becomes too steep for the novice and is recommended for intermediate and advanced skiers/shoers. Many skiers or snowshoers stop before the big ascent begins and head back at about 5.0 miles from the trailhead.

If you want a vigorous workout, keep going up the switchback trail; it's the road that cuts left and heads steeply east, and will take you another 2.5 miles to the top of the Outback Bowl Ski Lift. At the top of the Outback Bowl lift, you can either go back down the road the way you came or head down on the ski lift trail to the bottom of Keystone Gulch. Do keep in mind that if you choose the latter route, you'll be sharing the terrain with fast-moving downhill skiers and snowboarders.

From the trailhead ski or snowshoe along the Keystone Gulch Trail, which follows a four-wheel-drive road that heads south and then gently

Directions at a glance

- Park in plowed area off Keystone Gulch Road only! If no parking is available, park at the Keystone Lodge and take the free shuttle bus to the trailhead.

- Head south on Keystone Gulch Trail to the south and follow the old 4 x 4-vehicle road.

- Climb gently uphill for approximately 5.0 miles along this road until it cuts to the east and begins a steep ascent.

- Turn back here and enjoy gentle downhill glide/trek back to the trailhead.

Alternate route

- At approximately 5.0 miles from the trailhead, the road cuts off to the left and heads steeply east.

- Continue to climb the 2.5 miles of switchbacks to the top of the Outback Bowl Ski Lift.

- Return to the trailhead by skiing/shoeing back down the switchback road and then through Keystone Gulch, or by going on one of the marked downhill ski runs.

- At the bottom of the ski run, turn left and head north back through Keystone Gulch to the trailhead.

bends to the southeast. If you are a beginner, the first 5.0 miles are well suited to you because the trail climbs gradually through a heavily forested area and lacks hard turns. Though topographical maps should always be a part of your equipment, advanced map reading skills are not required here. Continue on the road, gaining more than 1,000 feet in elevation but don't fret, you'll have 5.0 miles to get acclimated to the higher elevation and to rest whenever you need to. The Keystone downhill area is right at your feet and above you to the southwest the magnificent Ten-Mile Mountain Range.

After the first 5.0 miles, the trail becomes more difficult because of a wide switchback that veers northeast and climbs steeply in elevation. If you are a novice, turn around at this point and head back downhill for a fun glide all the way to the trailhead. If you are an intermediate or advanced skier or snowshoer who wants a swift, fast climb, continue on, ascending more than 700 feet in just over 2.0 miles. Continue on the four-wheel-drive road to the east and watch for the Erickson Mine on the southwest side of Keystone Mountain. Remnants and structures should be visible across the valley to your right. Be aware that you'll often be above the timberline and won't be sheltered from the wind. At this higher elevation avalanche danger is more pronounced so please check with the Forestry Service for the latest avalanche information, especially if you plan on getting off the trail and doing some backcountry exploration on your own.

How to get there

From Denver take I–70 west approximately 80 miles. Take the Main Street exit to Dillon/Silverthorne. At the bottom of the off ramp, make a left onto U.S. Highway 6. Go east through Dillon. U.S. Highway 6 will curve back around Dillon Reservoir to the south. Follow the signs to Keystone—U.S. Highway 6 then heads southeast and then east. Look for the traffic light for the Keystone Ski Resort. Turn right at the traffic light marking the western entrance to the Keystone Ski Resort. Then make an immediate left and follow Keystone Road for 0.3 miles. At Soda Ridge Road turn right and follow it for 0.5 mile. Turn left onto the Keystone Gulch Road (marked with a Keystone street sign) and go 0.1 mile to the winter closure gate. Park in the plowed area. If there is not enough parking available, park at the Keystone Lodge and ride the free shuttle bus to the trailhead. If you're staying in Dillon, you can catch free, frequent shuttle buses from a variety of locations in town to the Keystone Resort and the trailhead. The Forest Service asks that you do not parallel park along Soda Ridge Road or park in any of the private drives.

Peru Creek

Montezuma, CO

Type of trail:	▬▬ ◉◉◉
Also used by:	Snowmobilers
Distance:	8.0 miles
Terrain:	Easy to moderately challenging climbs for beginners on main trail. Steep ascents and descents for the advanced skier/shoer on alternate route.
Trail difficulty:	Novice to advanced
Surface quality:	Ungroomed but often tracked by skiers/shoers.
Elevation:	Trailhead is at 10,030 feet and climbs to 11,061 feet at the Pennsylvania Mine.
Time:	3 to 5 hours
Avalanche danger:	Low on trail but increases at higher elevations
Snowmobile use:	Low to moderate
Food and facilities:	The Peru Creek trailhead is about 12.5 miles east of Dillon. Plan on staying in Dillon or at the Keystone Ski Resort. Information about lodging can be obtained from the Summit County Chamber of Commerce offices at (800) 530–3099. Or if you're planning on staying at the Keystone Ski Resort, call them at (800) 258–9553.
	Gas, groceries, water, and sack lunches should all be obtained before heading too far from Dillon or the Keystone Ski Resort. Once you get to the Peru Creek trailhead, there are no facilities.

If you are a novice skier or snowshoer who wants to take in the rich mining history of the area while enjoying a pleasant backcountry outing, the beginning part of this popular tour is well suited to you. Mine sites and remnants of old mining buildings whose stories are untold create a scenic foreground against the rugged mountains. In addition to a sack lunch and drinking water—taking your camera along is a must!

The Pennsylvania Mine, located at the end of this trail, was one of the better producers of silver ore in the area. Yielding high-quality silver ore, it was active from 1879 until the mid-1940s. If you are a more experienced skier or snowshoer, you may want to continue past the mine to the Horseshoe Basin or scout around the areas of Chihuahua and Ruby Gulches to the north. Be apprised that you'll cross potentially dangerous avalanche chutes and must call the Forest Service for the latest informa-

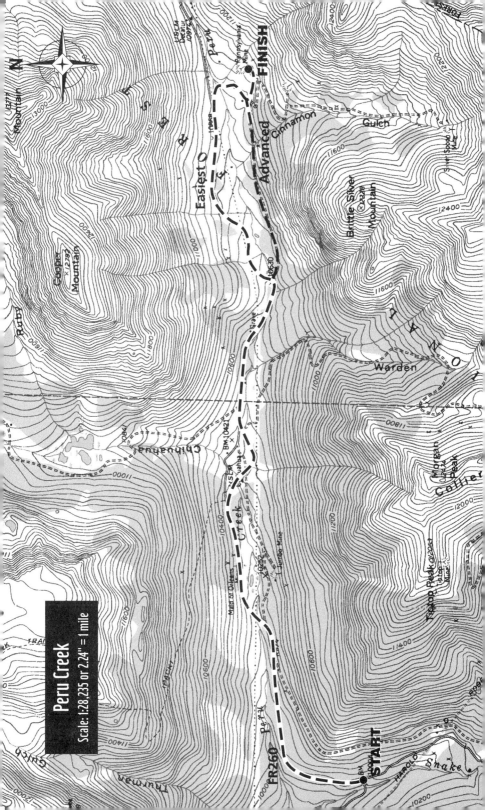

tion on danger levels. Back in 1898, the town of Decatur—which is located right on the trail—was completely destroyed by an avalanche slide off of Grays Peak! A good set of topo maps, avalanche beacons for everyone in the party, and snow shovels are highly recommended.

From the trailhead on FR 260, start skiing/snowshoeing north through a wooded area along the roadbed as it bends around the hillside. After about 0.5 mile, the road will take you east into Peru Creek Valley. Right away Morgan Peak at 12,474 feet is in view on your right, and soon afterward the snow-capped 12,782-foot peak of Cooper Mountain can be seen to the east.

The trail continues to climb steadily for the first 1.0 mile with grades upward of 28 percent. The trail forks, and the small trail heads off to the right. Stay on FR 260 and veer toward the left. After 1.5 mile, you'll see the remnants of the old Maid of Orleans Mine to your left, or north. Right below it to the south of the trail is the Jumbo Mine. A little farther on you'll reach the mouth of the Chihuahua Gulch where open meadows and steep ridges with avalanche chutes abound.

The route starts to climb more vigorously, and by the 2.0-mile point you'll already have ascended 400 feet to 10,421 feet. The trail veers south for a bit and then heads east again, climbing another 200 feet in and out of the trees for the next 1.0 mile. At about 2.75 miles from the trailhead— about 1.25 miles past the Maid of Orleans Mine—watch carefully for an old tombstone on the left side of the trail. The stone is old and weathered, but it's a one-hundred-year-old testament to many a miner who gave their lives seeking the riches of the Colorado Mountains. After 3.0 miles, you'll cross to the south side of Peru Creek and see a fork in the road.

The best route for novice and intermediate skiers/shoers is to stay on FR 260, which continues to the left toward Decatur. Go 1.0 mile and look for trail that cuts off to the right and heads south. This is the easiest way to the Pennsylvania Mine. The mine's mill still stands today and makes for a picturesque background.

If you're an advanced skier/shoer and want to really challenge yourself with some steep climbs and descents, take the right fork and climb steeply along Brittle Silver Mountain. The route offers up and down paths with grades of 40 percent to 50 percent and is not recommended for amateurs! Along this route after about the 4.0-mile mark, you'll pass Cinnamon Gulch and see the historic remnants of the Pennsylvania Mine.

Return to the trailhead along the same route and enjoy gentle glides/treks back down the 4.0-mile trail.

How to get there

From Denver go approximately 80 miles west on I–70 and take the Dillon/Silverthorne exit (205). At the bottom of the off-ramp, turn left and

Directions at a glance

- The Peru Creek trailhead is marked FR 260. Follow it north through aspen grove and then east into Peru Creek Valley.

- Trail forks at 1.0 mile from the trailhead. Stay on FR 260 and veer to the left.

- At 1.5-mile marker, you'll see the old Maid of Orleans Mine.

- Go 1 .25 miles past the Maid of Orleans Mine and look for the tombstone of a forgotten miner on the left side of the road.

- At about 3.0 miles from trailhead, the route forks. For the easiest route veer left and stay on FR 260.

- Go approximately 1.0 mile and look for trail that cuts off to the right and heads south.

- Take the trail to the right about 0.25 mile and look to your left—you should be able to see the remnants of the old abandoned Pennsylvania Mine and the mill that still stands today.

- To return, follow the same route back to the trailhead.

Alternate route

- At approximately 3.0 miles from the trailhead, the route splits. FR 260 continues to the left.

- The trail to the right heading east is designed for advanced skiers/shoers only!

- Lots of steep climbs and descents—upward of 40 to 50 percent grades along Brittle Silver Mountain.

- Trail continues along same path for approximately 1.0 mile and passes through Cinnamon Gulch.

- Trail ends about 0.25 mile below the old Pennsylvania Mill and mine.

- To return, follow the same route back to the trailhead.

head south on Highway 9. At about 0.5 mile, turn left on Highway 6, go through the town of Dillon, and follow the signs to Keystone. Stay on Highway 6 east, and approximately 1.6 miles past the intersection for the Keystone Ski Resort, which has a signal light, look for signs and right hand turn onto Montezuma Road (County Road 5). Continue on County Road 5 for 4.6 miles to the Peru Creek trailhead. It will be on your left and will be marked as Forest Road (FR) 260. The gate may be left open but please do not drive up this road. It is not passable. Park in the plowed area in front of the gate at FR 260.

Saints John

Montezuma, CO

Type of trail:	▬▬▬ ⬤
Also used by:	Snowmobilers
Distance:	5.2 miles
Terrain:	Short trail but steady and steep climbs.
Trail difficulty:	Novice to intermediate
Surface quality:	Ungroomed but often tracked by skiers/shoers.
Elevation:	Trail starts at 10,268 feet and ends at 11,500 feet.
Time:	3 to 5 hours
Avalanche danger:	Moderate—trail lies in path of avalanche chutes
Snowmobile use:	Moderate
Food and facilities:	The town of Montezuma, where the trailhead to the Saints John Trail and ghost town can be found, is about 13.5 miles east of Dillon. Plan on staying in Dillon or at the Keystone Ski Resort. Information about lodging can be obtained from the Summit County Chamber of Commerce offices at (800) 530–3099. Or if you're planning on staying at the Keystone Ski Resort, call them at (800) 258–9553.
	Gas, groceries, water, and sack lunches should all be obtained before heading too far from Dillon or the Keystone Ski Resort. Once you get to Montezuma and the trailhead, there are no facilities.

This trail is ideal for history buffs who love to wander over roads used more than a hundred years ago by miners seeking their fortunes in silver. The Saints John Mine, which dates back to 1863, was the site of the first major silver strike in Colorado. This valley, formed by glaciers, once thrived, having a library, sawmill, mill, and smelter. But no saloons! The town was named after Saint John the Baptist and Saint John the Evangelist. The townsite was partially destroyed in the 1800s by an avalanche, so skiers and snowshoers need to beware, and should contact the Forest Service for the latest on avalanche dangers along the trail.

Most of the time the danger level is low on the trail up to the old ghost town of Saints John but can become moderate after that. As always, and when heading into the backcountry, good topo maps, avalanche beacons for everyone in the party, and snow shovels should be considered standard equipment.

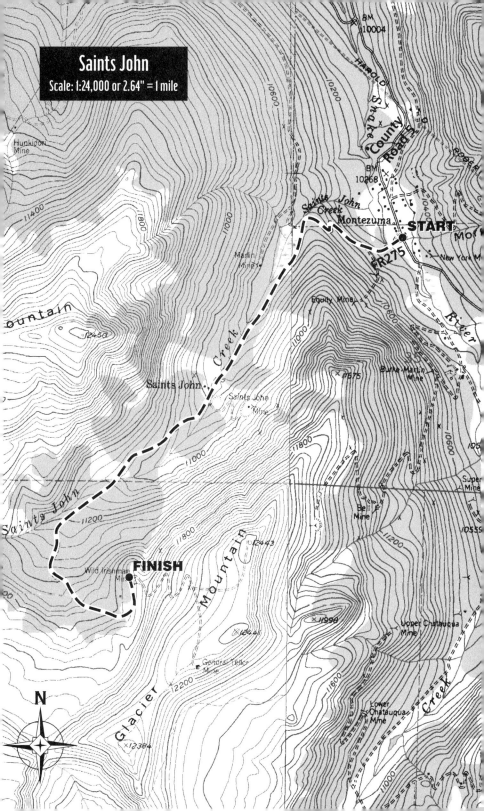

The Saints John Trail is short but also steep, gaining 1,400 feet in elevation in just about 2.5 miles. It is definitely for the outdoorperson in good physical shape. The end of the trail however rewards the hardy skier/snow shoer with spectacular views of two of Colorado's "Fourteeners"—the Grays Peak at 14,270 feet and the Torreys Peak at 14,267 feet.

From the trailhead, which is marked as Forest Road (FR) 275, follow Saints John Road through the actual townsite of Montezuma. Cross a bridge over the Snake River and begin climbing toward the northwest

Directions at a glance

- Saints John trailhead is marked as FR 275 and almost immediately there is a bridge crossing the Snake River.

- Head northwest on road through woods and past small road to left that leads to Equity Mine.

- Continue climb and switchbacking to the northwest for another 0.5 mile.

- Trail bends to the southwest and starts up the Saints John Creek Valley.

- Cross Saints John Creek at approximately 1.2-mile mark, and you'll see the remnants and structures of the Saints John townsite/ghost town.

- Beginners can turn around here and go back on the same trail.

Alternate routes

- After reaching Saints John townsite/ghost town, continue southwest on FR 275.

- At southwest edge of town, leave the road and drop down into the Saints John Creek bed to avoid possible avalanche chute.

- Traverse the creek bed for approximately 0.5 mile then climb back up and continue to follow the road.

- At approximately 2.5 miles, trail turns south and climbs steeply to the Wild Irishman Mine and the spectacular views of Grays Peak and Torreys Peak to the northeast.

through a forest. On your left at approximately 0.25 mile from the trail-head, you'll see a small road leading to the site of the old Equity Mine. Stay on FR 275 and continue northwest, switchbacking up a hill. Soon after you start your climb, you'll veer to the left or southwest, where you'll see the start of the Saints John Creek Valley. Continue heading southwest, climbing steadily, and meandering into and out of the woods and meadows. After the trail crosses over the Saints John Creek, you'll spot several old buildings of the abandoned Saints John townsite, 1.2 miles from Montezuma and the trailhead. A road off to the east leads to the actual mine. You are asked to respect that the structures here are privately owned.

This first half of the trail, which brings you into the old townsite, is rated for the novice. The second half of the route gets into more steep terrain and is better suited to the intermediate skier or snowshoer. If you are a beginner/novice, the townsite offers plenty of good photo opportunities and is an ideal location to enjoy a fast glide/trek back to the trailhead after lunch.

If you're planning on pressing on for the view of Grays and Torreys Peaks, after leaving the townsite of Saints John, it's advised that you drop down from the road itself and traverse along the Saints John Creek bed. This will help you to avoid a hazardous avalanche chute that's located just to the southwest of the town. After about 0.5 mile, you can return to the road and continue heading southwest and climbing for another 0.5 mile. The route takes you into the woods and out into open meadows. At about the 2.5-mile point, the road turns to the left or south and climbs more steeply until you're near treeline, then it veers to the north. The Wild Irishman Mine and indescribable views of two of Colorado's "Fourteeners" are just up ahead.

How to get there

From Denver go approximately 80 miles west on I–70 and take the Dillon/Silverthorne exit (205). At the bottom of the off-ramp, turn left and head south on Highway 9. At about 0.5 mile, turn left on Highway 6, go through the town of Dillon, and follow the signs to Keystone. Stay on Highway 6 east, and approximately 1.6 miles past the intersection for the Keystone Ski Resort, marked by a signal light, look for signs and make a turn onto Montezuma Road (County Road 5). Continue on CR 5 for 5.6 miles to the town of Montezuma. Park at the Saints John trailhead in the center of Montezuma.

Deer Creek

Montezuma, CO

Type of trail:	▬▬ 🥾
Also used by:	Snowmobilers
Distance:	5.2 miles
Terrain:	Nice slow and gentle climbs to end of trail.
Trail difficulty:	Novice
Surface quality:	Ungroomed but often tracked by skiers/shoers.
Elevation:	Trail starts at 10,600 feet and ends at 11,400 feet.
Time:	3 to 4 hours
Avalanche danger:	Low
Food and facilities:	Montezuma, where the trailhead to Deer Creek is, can be found 13.5 miles east of Dillon. Plan on staying in Dillon or at the Keystone Ski Resort. Information about lodging can be obtained from the Summit County Chamber of Commerce at (800) 530–3099. Or if you're planning on staying at the Keystone Ski Resort, call them at (800) 258–9553.

Gas, groceries, water, and sack lunches should all be obtained before heading too far from Dillon or the Keystone Ski Resort. Once you get to the townsite of Montezuma and then onto the Deer Creek trailhead, there are no facilities.

The Deer Creek Trail is a short, easy route for novice/beginner skiers or snowshoers who don't want the crowds they may encounter at the Saints John or Peru Creek Trails. Located at the end of Montezuma Road, the trail gets less use than the popular routes found throughout the area. If you want to be alone with the backcountry, Deer Creek is the answer. Laced with remnants of once bountiful silver mines, the trail offers much to look at in terms of mining history, and the four-wheel-drive road it follows is usually well tracked. Don't choose a windy day, though. Even though the tour is below treeline, the large, open clearings and meadows can make for a blustery outing.

From the end of the plowed road, the trailhead heads south immediately. Ski/shoe south and ignore the side roads that veer off to the east and west. Soon after getting on the trail, County Road 5 becomes Forest Road 5 and is designated as FR 5. Once past the old sawmill on your left, you'll begin to see evidence of the area's rich mining history with the Superior Mine to the west, the first of many along the route. A road goes

to the mine from the west, but you should avoid it. A lot of the mines though inactive are still privately owned, and you're asked to respect the rights of property owners.

Continue south on FR 5, which parallels Deer Creek, into a clearing and then back into the woods. At the 1.0-mile point, you'll pass Upper Chatauqua Mine; at the 1.5-mile point, you'll pass Lower Chatauqua Mine. You'll start to climb steadily, and by the 2.0-mile mark, you'll see the Star of the West Mine, the Arabella Mine, the Mohawk Mine, and the Upper and Lower Radical Mines off to the east. There are various roads going off to these historical remnants, but the best route to take is to follow Deer Creek to the southwest.

Continuing on, you'll meander into the trees and then out into clearings, climbing a little with 10 percent to 20 percent grades before the trail levels off. At about the 3.0-mile point when you're near timberline, you'll see the steep grades of the slopes to Radical Hill to your right and east. Although it's called Radical Hill, it's really a mountain with an elevation of 12,367 feet. To the west is Glacier Mountain, which towers to a height of 12,441 feet. Sculpted by forceful winds, these massive cliffs of snow take your breath away.

If you are a beginning skier or shoer, this is the spot to turn around. To return to the trailhead, just go back the way you came and enjoy the slight downhill grade.

How to get there

From Denver go approximately 80 miles west on I–70 and take the Dillon/Silverthorne exit (205). At the bottom of the off-ramp, turn left and head south on Highway 9. At about 0.5 mile, turn left on Highway 6, go

Directions at a glance

- Depending on where the snow closure area is, the Deer Creek trailhead begins at the end of the plowed road and heads south. Look for trail signs for FR 5.

- Pass the sawmill on your left or east side, and you'll start to see remnants and structures of old abandoned mines.

- Trail continues to follow FR 5 along Deer Creek with gentle 10 percent to 20 percent grades.

- At about the 3.0-mile point, the trail begins to climb steeply. For the beginner/novice skier or shoer, it's time to turn around and enjoy the gentle downhill trip back to the trailhead.

through the town of Dillon, and follow the signs to Keystone. Stay on Highway 6 east, and approximately 1.6 miles past the intersection that would take you to the Keystone Ski Resort, look for signs and turn right onto Montezuma Road (County Road 5). Continue on CR 5 for 5.6 miles to the town of Montezuma. Park at the Saints John trailhead in the center of Montezuma. Or if the road is open, continue to the southern end of Montezuma.

Mesa Cortina

Dillon, CO

Type of trail:	▬▬ ●
Distance:	7.0 miles
Terrain:	Gentle climbs and gradual ascents.
Trail difficulty:	Novice to intermediate
Surface quality:	Ungroomed but sometimes tracked by skiers/shoers.
Elevation:	Trail starts at 9,200 feet and ends at 9,560 feet.
Time:	3 to 5 hours
Avalanche danger:	First 3.5 miles, low; after that and at the higher elevations extreme avalanche danger exists.
Food and facilities:	This trail is located just outside the city limits of Dillon. There are plenty of hotels, motels, grocery stores, convenience stores, and fast-food outlets less than ten minutes from the trailhead. Because the trail goes into the Eagle's Nest Wilderness Area, there are no facilities found on the trail itself. Pack in your lunches, drinks, etc.—and pack out your trash!

The Mesa Cortina Trail is an excellent choice for beginners because the route follows terrain that is very gentle and gradual. Overall elevation change from the trailhead to the turnaround point is less than 360 vertical feet over 3.5 miles. What can make this route tricky is that it's not too well marked, and after a fresh snowfall, when you have to break the trail, it can be difficult to follow. Carrying a good set of topographic maps of the area should be considered a must. Dense tree cover and the trek through parts of the Eagle's Nest Wilderness Area, though, make this a unique outdoor experience. Views of Silverthorne and Ptarmigan Mountains and Lake Dillon all add to the splendor.

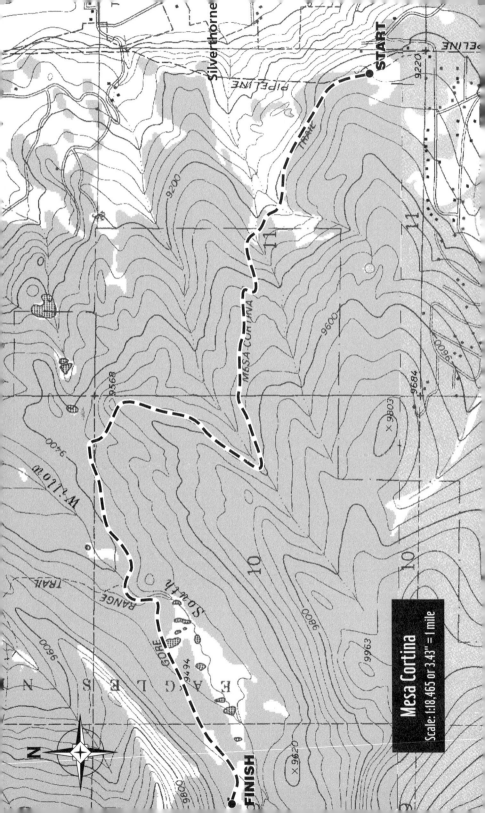

Mesa Cortina
Scale: 1:18,465 or 3.43" = 1 mile

From the trailhead ski north through groves of aspen and meadows dotted with sagebrush. You'll peek out over the Blue River Valley and continue on, bending around to the northwest. At the edge of a lodgepole pine forest, you'll officially enter the Eagle's Nest Wilderness Area. The trail becomes part of an old logging road and switchbacks over a hill through a thick canopy of trees. Skiing north and then veering to the northwest, you'll go down a hill and see a four-wheel-drive vehicle trail come in from the east at a little over the 2.0-mile mark. A short distance ahead is South Willow Creek, a good spot to relax and listen to the quaking sounds of the aspens or breathe in the scent of the pines. The creek originates behind Buffalo Mountain to the southwest, rushing down between the Buffalo's mighty 12,777-foot peak and Red Peak's 13,189-foot pinnacle.

> ## Directions at a glance
>
> - Trailhead is on the right side of Aspen Drive.
>
> - Take the trail north and northwest through groves of trees for approximately 2.0 miles.
>
> - Here the trail will intersect a jeep trail coming in from the east.
>
> - Stay on the trail to the northwest until crossing South Willow Creek.
>
> - Across the creek the Mesa Cortina Trail intersects with the Wheeler–Gore Trail.
>
> - Go left on Wheeler–Gore Trail along South Willow Creek for approximately 1.0 mile.
>
> - Rest here before turning around. Do not go into the dangerous avalanche area beyond.
>
> - Return to the trailhead via the same route, and you'll enjoy gentle downhill trekking or skiing.

Cross over the creek. Here the trail joins with the Wheeler–Gore Range Trail. Take the trail that goes to your left (the Wheeler-Gore Trail), and for 1.0 mile you'll ski or snowshoe up a hill to the upper end of a flat valley. The trail basically follows the route of South Willow Creek. At 9,560 feet, this meadow makes for a fun picnicking spot and turnaround area.

Beyond this meadow are extremely dangerous avalanche paths created by the steep slopes of Buffalo Mountain. Travel is definitely not recommended!

How to get there

From I–70 take exit 205 (the freeway exit for Dillon/Silverthorne) and head north on Colorado 9. Go north and then turn left onto Wildernest Road at the first intersection past the highway interchange. (Wendy's restaurant will be on your right.) Take Wildernest Road for 0.2 miles then turn right onto Adams Avenue. Almost immediately turn left onto the

Photo by John Kelly, courtesy of Aspen Skiing Company

Royal Buffalo Mountain Road (County Road 1240). Go 0.8 miles on Royal Buffalo and take a sharp right onto Lakeview Drive. Proceed 0.5 miles and turn left onto Aspen Drive. Travel a short distance to parking on the left and the trailhead on your right.

Lily Pad Lake

Lily Pad Lake, Frisco, CO

Type of trail:	
Distance:	3.0 miles
Terrain:	Gentle grades and lots of flat open forest areas.
Trail difficulty:	Easy/beginner
Surface quality:	Ungroomed but usually tracked by skiers/shoers.
Elevation:	Trail starts at about 9,500 to 9,600 feet
Time:	1 to 3 hours
Avalanche danger:	Low
Food and facilities:	There's a good selection of hotels, motels, and restaurants in the town of Frisco. Hotel recommendations include the Sky Vue, the Wood Inn, and the Creekside. The latter two are exceptional bed-and-breakfast facilities. Information on restaurants and accommodations can be obtained by calling the Summit County Chamber of Commerce Association (800) 530–3099.
	Gas, groceries, sack lunches, and drinks can also be found in Frisco, and it's recommended that you stock up before leaving town. You won't find facilities or food on the Lily Pad Lake Trail.

This is a popular trail for skiers/snowshoers in the Dillon/Silverthorne area because it enters the Eagles Nest Wilderness Area, and no mechanized vehicles or snowmobiles are allowed there. Ideal for beginners, the trail is pleasant for even the most inexperienced skier and shoer. The Lily Pad Lake Trail is short, has the gentlest of grades, and meanders around forests of spruce and aspen to wind up at the pristine, frozen lake. Too shallow for ice fishing, Lily Pad Lake is ideal for picnicking and picture taking.

Surrounded by beaver ponds, the area was a favorite for fur trappers in the early 1800s. Gold was reported to the north in the Salt Lick Gulch

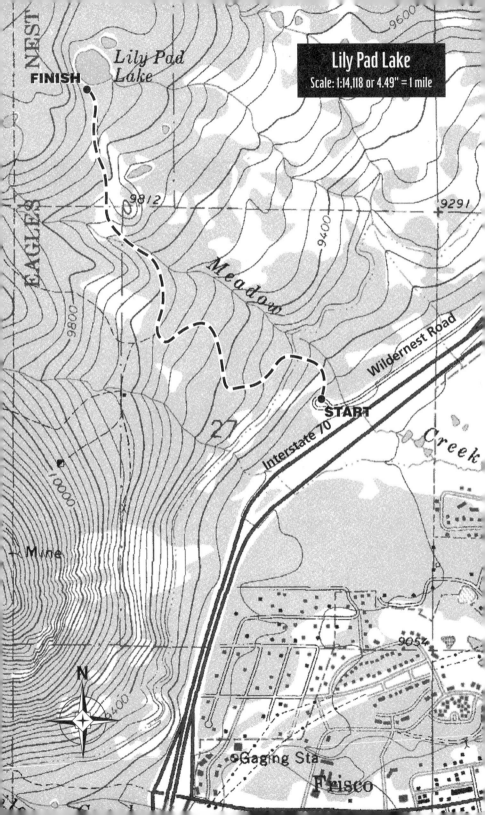

NEST

Lily Pad
Lake

FINISH

Lily Pad Lake
Scale: 1:14,118 or 4.49" = 1 mile

9812

9291

EAGLES

9800

Meadow

9400

Wildernest Road

START

Creek

27

Interstate 70

10000

9054

Mine

N

9400

9600

Gaging Sta

Frisco

area by a pioneer who told everyone that he had found "gold dust" in the mouth of a deer he had just shot for food. When the word got around, hordes of miners arrived, and the Salt Lick Gulch area became an important mining center. Like so many of the reported "get-rich-quick" mining areas, those who came and mined the Salt Lick went home licking their financial wounds.

Today the area is a beginner skier/shoer's paradise. From the Lily Pad trailhead, you'll start at the Wildernest subdivision. You'll encounter a climb to the water tank that services the homes, and if you are a novice skier, you might find it intimidating. The maximum grade is less than 20 percent, and during that first 0.5 mile, you'll only gain about 414 feet. If you are a beginner, you need to take it easy and realize that once you're on top, the rest of the trail is a breeze!

After cresting the first big hill, go south and southwest through lodgepole pines and dense aspen stands. The trail then turns north and then west. Each leg is only about an eighth of a mile. At about 0.75 mile from the trailhead, look for another trail that intersects the Lily Lake Trail on your right, or from the north. Take the trail to the right. There should be Forest Service signage indicating that this is the trail to the Lily Pad Lake area. Another .75 mile of gentle ascent and you'll arrive at Lily Pad Lake.

Directions at a glance

- Look for a ROAD CLOSED sign and a wire cable at the trailhead to Lily Pad Lake.

- Go west on trail and plan for steep climb during the first 0.25 to 0.50 mile.

- Trail levels out to nearly flat ground on top.

- At about 0.75 mile, look for signage to Lily Pad Lake. Trail will cut off to your right and go another 0.75 mile to the lake.

- Return to the trailhead by following the same trail back down and enjoy the gentle downhill glide or trek.

How to get there

From Denver take I–70 west approximately 75 miles, and then take the Silverthorne/Dillon exit (205) to Colorado Highway 9. Go north on Colorado Highway 9. The first traffic light past the I–70 interchange is the intersection of Wildernest Road and Tanglewood Road. Turn left and continue past the Wildernest Hospitality Center. Follow this road until it ends at a large loop. Park at the end of the loop, unload your gear, and trek back up to the ROAD CLOSED sign and wire cable. Look for the big water tank on the hill in front of you. The Lily Pad Lake Trail begins here.

North Ten Mile

Frisco, CO

Type of trail:	▬▬▬ ⬮⬮⬮
Also used by:	Snowmobilers for first 2.5 miles
Distance:	10.0 miles
Terrain:	Steep climb at the beginning and then gentle to moderate climbs to trail's end.
Trail difficulty:	Intermediate
Surface quality:	Ungroomed but usually well tracked by skiers/shoers.
Elevation:	9,400 feet at trailhead to 10,250 feet at trail's end
Time:	5 hours to full day
Avalanche danger:	Low
Snowmobile use:	Moderate
Food and facilities:	There's a good selection of hotels, motels, and restaurants in the town of Frisco. The closest overnight accommodations to the Ten Mile Trail are in the Frisco area. Hotel recommendations include the Sky Vue, the Wood Inn, or the Creekside. The latter two are exceptional bed-and-breakfast facilities. Information on restaurants and accommodations can be obtained by calling the Summit County Chamber of Commerce Association (800) 530–3099.

Gas, groceries, sack lunches, and drinks can also be found in Frisco. Stock up before leaving town. You won't find facilities or food on the Ten Mile Trail.

The valley of the North Ten Mile Creek area is a haven for snowmobilers in the winter months, but don't let that discourage you. At about 2.5 miles from the trailhead, your ski/snowshoe route will enter the Eagle's Nest Wilderness Area, where no mechanized vehicles are allowed. You're then alone with canyons carved millions of years ago from glaciers and the towering snow-capped peaks of Wichita Mountain, at 10,855 feet, and Chief Mountain, at 10,880 feet. Finally, you'll see the Gore Mountain Range to the west.

From the trailhead, head west. The first 0.5 mile of the trail is somewhat intimidating and exhilarating because of a steep climb up into the trees. You'll gain just over 900 feet in vertical elevation during that first 0.5 mile. If you are snowshoeing, definitely plan on carrying ski poles; if you are skiing, you should have "skins" for the steep ascent that can be upward of 40 percent for short distances.

Once you've made the "big climb," the ground levels off to a gradual ascent of little more than a 2 to 7 percent grade. For the next 2.0 miles or so, you'll glide or trek past numerous beaver ponds, wood thickets, and the remnants of old mines. In the early part of the century, miners used this trail to cart out thousands of pounds of gold and silver ore. Snow-covered tailing mounds can be seen dotting the landscape.

Continue through meadows and past another pond, and then you'll meander in and out of glades of aspen and pine. This area is a popular touring region for snowmobilers so tracks are likely to be heading off in all directions. Ignore all the sidetracks and continue heading west, following the North Ten Mile Creek.

At about the 2.5-mile point, you'll enter the Eagle's Nest Wilderness Area, home to snowshoe hares, fox, coyotes, and other winter wildlife. Look for U.S. Forest Service's wooden signs that are posted at this point. They'll tell you that you are entering a designated wilderness area, and

Directions at a glance

- Trailhead for the North Ten Mile Creek route begins at the west end of the parking area. Exit the parking lot and onto the trail heading west. Expect that first 0.5 mile is going to be steep (30–45%) uphill grade.

- After first 0.5 mile trail levels out and continues with very gentle ascent for next 2.0-plus miles.

- At approximately 2.5 miles, you'll enter the Eagles Nest Wilderness Area. Look for signs and the end of motorized traffic.

- At about 3.5 miles from the trailhead, look for the intersection of the Gore Range Trail that runs north to south and across the North Ten Mile Creek Trail.

- This is a good point to turn around and go back, otherwise it's another 1.5 miles up the trail to the northwest. Steep, snow-capped mountains border the trail to the west.

- To return to the trailhead, follow the same trail back to the east that you skied/shoed in on.

- For the last 0.5-mile enjoy the downhill that you climbed up on your way in!

it's at this point that no mechanized vehicles are allowed. It's also to this area that red-tailed hawks and golden eagles return to spend the warmer late-winter and early-spring months. And even though the snows are still deep on the ground, these residents come home to roost and provide some great photo opportunities.

The trail takes you past several clearings, and you'll continue west (straight) through more forest. At about the 3.5-mile point, you'll come to the junction of the Gore Range Trail. Shoeing and skiing opportunities abound by going left or right, but to complete this trail you'll need to keep going west on the Ten Mile Creek Trail and enjoy the more level skiing that will lead you into a flat and open valley. Views of the Gore Range Mountains are ahead and they are magnificent. You may wish to use this as a resting area and a turn back. However, if you want to go on, you'll see that the trail contours northwest until the valley ends beside steep snowy slopes. For the return trip, just head east on the trail and enjoy the downhill grade. The trip should go fast. And remember that last 0.5 mile to the trailhead that was such a steep climb at the beginning will now be a challenging downhill descent.

How to get there

From Denver take I–70 west approximately 80 miles to the Frisco Main Street exit, 201. Immediately after exiting the freeway, turn west into a plowed parking area. The trailhead is located immediately off the interstate exit on the north side.

Vail Pass to Shrine Pass

Vail Pass, Vail, CO

Type of trail:	▬▬ ●
Also used by:	Snowmobilers
Distance:	5.1 miles to and from Shrine Mountain Pass
	6.0 miles to and from the Shrine Mountain Inn cabins
	22 miles to and from Redcliff
Terrain:	Gentle grades and lots of flat open forest areas.
Trail difficulty:	Beginner to intermediate
Surface quality:	Ungroomed but usually tracked by skiers/shoers.
Elevation:	Trail begins at 10,580 feet and ends at the town of Redcliff at 8,680 feet.
Time:	3 to 5 hours to the Pass and the Cabins. All day to Redcliff and back.
Avalanche danger:	Low
Snowmobile use:	Moderate to heavy
Food and facilities:	Vail is only 10 miles to the west. It's a great place to play and stay, offering luxury hotels, reasonably priced motels, bed-and-breakfasts, and budget condos. For information on the over sixty different lodging options, call Vail/Beaver Creek Central Reservations (800–525–2257). Make sure you get your groceries, sack lunches, and drinks before leaving Vail. Food is not available once you get up onto Vail Pass.
	The Shrine Mountain Inn consists of three cabins—Jay's, Chuck's, and Walter's. Each can accommodate up to twelve overnight guests and is operated by the Tenth Mountain Division Hut Association. Information on the cabins and reservations can be made by calling (303) 925–5775.

Unlike most other areas found throughout Colorado that are open and free to the public for skiing and snowshoeing, the Vail Pass is now part of a "fee demonstration area." It's one in which you have to pay a user fee, and the money collected will be used to manage this heavy-use area. Self-fee tubes are available at all access points to the area. For information about the fees, call the Holy Cross Forest Service district office at (970) 827–5715.

The Shrine Pass Trail is so named because of its spectacular views of the Mount of the Holy Cross, so named because of the snow-covered cross that is emblazoned on the side of the mountain, immortalized in

writings by Ralph Waldo Emerson. The trail has many attractions: It follows a wide and heavily used dirt road and a creek so you don't need advanced map-reading skills. It has 9.0 miles of downhill and so goes relatively quickly. And it's so popular that it is usually always tracked. If you are a novice skier or snowshoer, you'll be able to stretch yourself with a longer journey, but not necessarily a more difficult one. The first 2.0 miles offer a workout with moderate uphill climbs. The rest of the journey is pleasantly downhill. Do however be aware that the trail is also very popular with snowmobilers and so care must be taken to stay out of each other's way.

After paying your user fee at the trailhead, you start the trail with two treeless switchbacks uphill that eventually curve to the southwest. The steady climb continues, and you veer to the northwest for the next 1.0 mile. The road then levels off for 0.5 mile or so and takes you in a more northern direction toward the pass. You pass near the top of Black Lakes

Directions at a glance

- Trailhead begins at the parking lot (pay your day-use fee!) and climbs gently for first 2.0 miles, beginning with two treeless switchbacks.
- At just over 2.5 miles from the trailhead, you'll reach the Shrine Pass.
- At about 2.7 miles from the trailhead, road to the left will lead you to the Shrine Mountain Inn.
- If going to the cabins, take the trail to the left and go 0.3 mile to the cabins.
- Return to the trailhead by going back the same route.

Alternate route

- If you're not planning on going to the Shrine Mountain Inn and want to continue on to the town of Redcliff, stay on the Shrine Pass Road.
- Approximately 0.5 mile up from the cut off to the cabins, you'll be able to see the Mount of the Holy Cross. Watch for the signs and the overlook.
- Continue on the road and you'll ski/shoe along the north side of Turkey Creek.
- Trail ends in small town of Redcliff.
- To return to the trailhead, it's 11.0 miles back on the same route.

Ridge then descend gently over a meadow. You've reached the summit of Shrine Pass at 11,089 feet.

Once you cross the summit, you have a myriad of options. If you've had enough of a journey and don't want to spend all day on the trail, you can head back to the trailhead the way you came. Or you can go left, heading southwest for 0.3 mile along a well-traversed road into glades of trees to the Shrine Mountain Inn. Privately owned, the inn is a part of the Tenth Mountain Division Hut Association and is a fun place for an overnight—or longer—stay. There are vast areas of deep powder here where you can have fun in the backcountry. The inn itself is made up of three cabins: Jay's, Chuck's, and Walter's. The cost for staying overnight with advance reservations is $35 per person. That's a little more expensive than most of the other cabins, huts, and yurts throughout Colorado, but these fancy cabins are complete with running water, showers, electricity, and a sauna. If you're planning on stopping off at the cabins for day use, you'll find that there is an additional day-use fee. You can make reservations through the Tenth Mountain Division Hut Association (303–925–5775).

If you're not going to the Shrine Mountain Inn and plan on continuing to Redcliff, keep on the Shrine Pass Road, heading northwest. The descent will start at the head of the Turkey Creek drainage where the valley curves to the west. At the 3.25-mile point you can rest and enjoy the endless vistas of the Mount of the Holy Cross at an overlook. (There are signs and toilet facilities here for your convenience.)

Continuing on the road, you'll ski along the north side of Turkey Creek, around open meadows, and then in and out of woods, descending gradually. Over the next several miles, you'll cross over Turkey Creek and pass a bridge to Wearyman Creek and a water tank before you eventually enter the city of Redcliff. The trail ends almost at the back door of a small restaurant in Redcliff. It's a good spot to have a cup of coffee or a bite to eat before heading back to the trailhead, reversing your route.

How to get there

From Denver go west on I–70 approximately 90 miles to the Vail Pass exit. If you're coming from Vail, take I 70 east for about 10 miles and exit at Vail Pass. Immediately after getting off the freeway, you'll see a large parking lot on the west side of the interstate. It's kept plowed all winter, and it has a rest stop and a warming hut.

Commando Run to Vail

Vail Pass, Vail, CO

Type of trail:	▰▰▰▰ ⬤
Also used by:	Snowmobilers for first 4 miles; downhill skiers last 2 miles at Vail Ski Resort.
Distance:	18 miles (one-way only trail; leave shuttle vehicle at base of Vail Ski Resort)
Terrain:	Challenging steep climbs and descents.
Trail difficulty:	Advanced/expert
Surface quality:	Ungroomed backcountry and usually well tracked by skiers/shoers.
Elevation:	Vail Pass trailhead at 10,580 feet; Vail Ski area at 8,331 feet
Time:	One full day
Avalanche danger:	Moderate
Snowmobile use:	Moderate to heavy for first 4.0 miles, then none
Food and facilities:	Vail, only 10 miles west, is a great place to play and stay. Luxury hotels, reasonably priced motels, bed-and-breakfasts, and budget condos are available. For information on the more than 60 different lodging options, call Vail/Beaver Creek Central Reservations (800–525–2257). Make sure you get your groceries, sack lunches, and drinks before leaving Vail. There's no place to buy food once you get up onto Vail Pass. Ski and shoe rentals/repairs can be taken care of at the Nordic Center, located at the Vail Golf Course Clubhouse (970–845–5313). Guides for the Commando Run are also available through the Vail Nordic Center.

The Commando Run from Vail Pass back to the Vail Ski Resort is regarded as one of the most challenging and best ski/snowshoe runs in Colorado. The Commando Run is named for the U.S. Army's Tenth Mountain Division soldiers who used to train along this demanding route for high-altitude skiing combat and commando raids during World War II. Popular today for its outstanding views and quality of snow, it's often tracked and can be accomplished in one full, hardy day of skiing.

Commando Run gets its advanced/expert rating for several reasons. The tour is long and the terrain is difficult. Map- and compass-reading skills are a must, and a good handheld GPS receiver can help you stay on course. Even though many parts of the route are well defined, skiers will encounter sections along ridgelines that are not marked, where it's easy

Commando Run to Vail
Scale: 1:111,111 or 0.57" = 1 mile

START

Vail
Vail Ski
Resort

Interstate 70

Two Elks Pass

Siberia Peak

Bartle Mountain

EAGLE CO
SUMMIT CO

to go off in the wrong direction. If you are an experienced skier/shoer, however, the tour is an enjoyable test of stamina and technique. If you're not sure you want to tackle the Commando Run without a little help, you may want to consider arranging for a guide through the Vail Nordic Center (970–845–5313).

Start at the Vail Pass trailhead, skiing along Shrine Pass Road, climbing over two sets of treeless switchbacks. This puts you into the woods about 2.0 miles from the trailhead. The route veers to the northwest. At about 2.5 miles, the road that cuts off to the left would lead you to the Shrine Mountain Inn cabins. At about 2.7 miles, you'll descend through a meadow and find yourself at the top of Shrine Mountain Pass at an elevation of 11,089 feet. Look for the signs.

Continue on Shrine Pass Road northwest and start descending at the head of the Turkey Creek drainage where the valley carves to the west. Pass the Mount of the Holy Cross overlook, skiing on the north side of Turkey Creek. At about the 4.0-mile point from the trailhead, the trail intersects Timber Creek Road (designated FR 712) in a clearing. Take this road to the right, or north, climbing for 0.5 mile to the northwest. Soon this road forks and you should take Lime Creek Road, which veers to the left or west. Entering the woods you'll start to climb steeply to Battle Mountain, elevation 11,611 feet. Continue west once on top of the ridge. At about the 6.0-mile point, contour north, climbing again to another elevation point of 11,710 feet. Take a breather and look out over the endless views.

Ski along the top of the ridge, first northwest and then northeast, and then you'll encounter a sharp descent down the forested ridge, heading north and ending at Two Elks Pass. Just to the northwest you can see the back bowls of the Vail downhill ski area. Climb north over the open, often windy south face of Siberia Peak, elevation 11,816 feet, and then descend down the northeast ridge, heading west and to Mill Creek. Here you'll begin a steep downhill drop into an area called the Mushroom Bowl. At the bottom of this bowl, to the north, you'll see Mill Creek Road. Ski west along this road for about 2.5 miles to the Vail Ski Resort area. Beyond the Golden Peak lift, you'll arrive at the downhill slopes where you can choose from a myriad of different runs to reach the base.

How to get there

From Denver take I–70 west approximately 90 miles to the Vail Pass exit. From Vail take I–70 east for 10 miles and get off at the Vail Pass exit. There is a large parking lot west of the interstate that is plowed all winter and has a rest stop and a warming hut. (There's a day-use fee. Please pay it.) Since it's a one-way trip from Vail Pass down to the Vail Ski Resort, make sure that you leave a shuttle car at the base of the ski resort. Or make arrangements for a shuttle service in Vail to bring you back to your vehicle on top of Vail Pass.

Directions at a glance

- The trailhead begins at the parking lot and climbs gently for first 2.0 miles, beginning with two treeless switchbacks.

- At about 2.7 miles from the trailhead, road to the left cuts off to the Shrine Mountain Inn.

- Approximately 0.5 mile up from the cutoff to the cabins, you'll be able to see the Mount of the Holy Cross. Watch for the signs and the overlook.

- Continue on the trail and you'll ski/shoe along the north side of Turkey Creek.

- At about the 4.0-mile point, trail intersects with Timber Creek Road (FR 712).

- Take Timber Creek Road to the right, climb for 0.5 mile north and northwest.

- When Timber Creek Road forks, take the route to the left (Lime Creek Road) and head west. Look for Battle Mountain to your west and north. Climb to ridgeline at 11,611 feet.

- At about the 6.0-mile point, begin contouring north and climb again to 11,710 feet.

- Ski along the ridge northwest and then northeast until you drop down along forested ridge area.

- Continue north and cross at Two Elks Pass.

- Continue north climbing Siberia Peak and then descend down the northeast ridge.

- At the bottom of Siberia Peak, you'll pick up Mill Creek Trail. Continue downhill through the Mushroom Bowl heading west. Trail turns into Mill Creek Road.

- Continue west and northwest for approximately 2.5 miles to the Vail Ski Resort.

Corral Creek

Vail Pass, Vail, CO

Type of trail:	▬▬ ⬭
Also used by:	Snowmobilers
Distance:	5.0-mile loop
Terrain:	Moderate climb to an area with lots of open descents.
Trail difficulty:	Beginner to intermediate
Surface quality:	Ungroomed but often well tracked by skiers/shoers.
Elevation:	Trail starts at 10,549 feet; highest elevation is at 11,000 feet.
Time:	3 to 4 hours
Avalanche danger:	Low to moderate
Snowmobile use:	Moderate
Food and facilities:	Vail, 10 miles to the west, is a great place to play and stay. Luxury hotels, reasonably priced motels, bed-and-breakfasts, and budget condos are available. For information call the Vail/Beaver Creek Central Reservations (800–525–2257). Make sure you get your groceries, sack lunches, and drinks before leaving Vail. Food is not available once you get up onto Vail Pass.

I f you want to get an early start cross-country skiing or snowshoeing, this is a great trail because it is in one of the areas that gets lots of snow early—sometimes as early as November. Here you can enjoy the backcountry without actually being too distant from the city. The Corral Creek Trail is on the east side of I–70, and it's a sweet and relatively easy alternative to the Shrine Pass Trail to the west, one that gets so much snowmobile and skier usage. Corral Creek is a favorite with the locals who want to get out and not put up with the more crowded areas to the west.

With a 10 percent-graded hill right at the start, this is a good trail if you are a beginner skier/shoer who wants to hit it hard at first and then have a pleasant tour with gradual changes in elevation. From the parking lot cross over to the east side of I–70. The trail is not well marked so don't expect to see much more than other ski/shoe tracks heading northeast and climbing steadily up and around the hill. For the first 0.3 mile as you climb the hill, you'll gain about 300 vertical feet in elevation.

Crest or side-hike the hill around to the northeast. Below you is the Corral Creek drainage area. There is plenty of open country in the

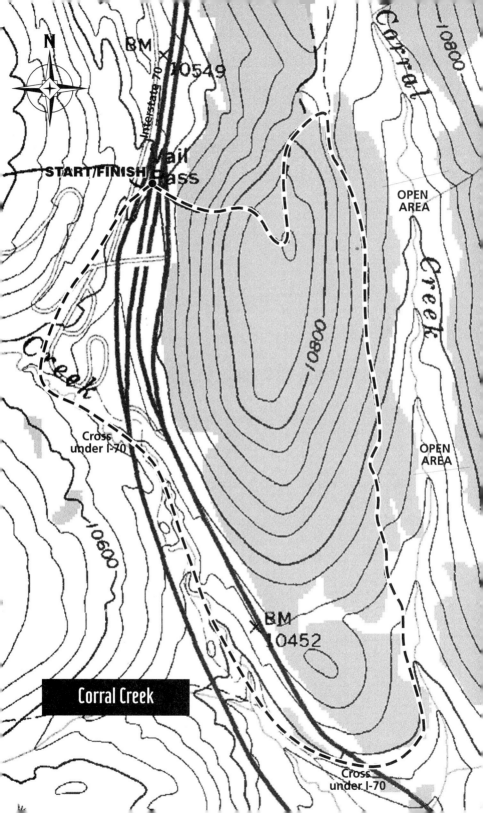

N

BM ✕ 10549

START/FINISH

Vail Pass

OPEN AREA

Corral

Creek

Creek

Cross under I-70

10600

OPEN AREA

BM ✕ 10452

Corral Creek

Cross under I-70

10800

10800

drainage both to the north and south. The Corral Creek Trail itself actually is the one that bends around to the south, following the creek. Here you can take advantage of the open and wide slopes of the drainage to practice carving turns, enjoy a downhill snowshoe jaunt, or unpack your snowboard and go for it! Feel free to ski off the trail, selecting any route you want to best explore the area. As long as you keep heading south, down the Corral Creek drainage area, you'll eventually loop around, and at the 2.75-mile point the trail hits its lowest point and actually crosses back under I–70.

The trail divides quite literally between the north and south divided interstate. Catch the road heading north, paralleling the interstate and running in between the traffic above, and begin a gradual ascent for its last 1.5 miles. The trail ends right back at the parking lot on the west side of the interstate where you left your vehicle!

How to get there

From Denver go west on I–70 approximately 90 miles to the Vail Pass exit. If you're coming from Vail, take I–70 east for about 10 miles and exit at Vail Pass. Immediately after getting off the freeway, you'll see a large parking lot on the west side of the interstate. It's kept plowed all winter, and it has a rest stop and a warming hut.

Unlike most other areas found throughout Colorado that are open and free to the public for skiing and snowshoeing, the Vail Pass is now part of a "fee demonstration area." It's one in which you have to pay a user fee, and the money collected will be used to manage this heavy-use area. Self-fee tubes are available at all access points to the area. For information about the fees, call the Holy Cross Forest Service district office at (970) 827–5715.

Directions at a glance

- Trail begins in the parking lot on the west side of I–70. (Pay your day-use fee!)

- Cross over to the east side of I–70.

- Climb hill to the northeast.

- When you've reached the ridge, you'll see the large open Corral Creek drainage area.

- Trail tracks downhill to the south.

- At 2.75-mile trail crosses back under I–70.

- Take trail to the north, staying between north and southbound traffic of interstate for approximately 1.5 mile.

- Trail turns into a road and will bring you back to the parking lot where you left your car.

Boreas Pass

Boreas Pass, Breckenridge, CO

Type of trail:	▬▬ ⬤
Also used by:	Snowmobilers
Distance:	7.2 miles to and from Baker's Tank; or 13.4 miles to and from the Boreas Summit and Section House hut
Terrain:	Moderate climbs along old railroad bed all the way from the trailhead to the summit.
Trail difficulty:	Easy to moderate
Surface quality:	Ungroomed but usually well tracked by skiers/shoers.
Elevation:	Trailhead at 10,229 feet, climbs to 11,481 feet; elevation change 1,140 feet
Time:	4 hours to all day
Avalanche danger:	Low
Snowmobile use:	Moderate
Food and facilities:	No facilities along the trail. For day trips, bring food, sack lunches, snacks, and water from Breckenridge. Plenty of grocery stores, convenience stores, and fast-food restaurants in town. If you're planning to stay over at the Section House hut, bring food and sleeping bags with you. The Tenth Mountain Division Hut Association takes care of the rest of the basic amenities. Advance reservations are a must and can be made by calling the association for more information at (970) 925–5775.

Boreas Pass was originally built as a wagon train road and was later used as the route for the nation's highest elevation, narrow-gauge railroad. From 1872 to 1938, a host of specially designed locomotives clanked along the tracks, handled the high altitudes, and ascended high grades and tight curves. In its time it provided one of the most important means of transportation across the Continental Divide.

Today the remnants of the route provide winter enthusiasts with great cross-country skiing and snowshoeing opportunities. In this best of all worlds, you'll experience the joy of skiing and shoeing into and out of glade after glade of spruce, aspen, and fir trees. You'll also get an opportunity to traverse along a south-facing sunny route that travels alongside the railroad bed and offers a gentle 3 percent grade. This route is ideal if you are a beginning snowshoer or cross-country skier.

Boreas Pass

Scale: 1:38,095 or 1.66" = 1 mile

START

FINISH

Section House Hut

N

Photo by Biege Jones, courtesy of Aspen Skiing Company

Just opened up is a new hut at the summit. Called the Section House, the hut is named in honor of the railroad workers from days gone by who took care of this "section of track." The Section House is a structure that is 115 years old and has been fully restored to its original splendor by the U.S. Forest Service. Today it is once again a 2,000-square-foot, two-story hewn log structure. Many more modern accommodations and facilities than were found over 100 years ago have been built into the renovation, and today it can accommodate up to twelve skiers/snowshoers for an overnight visit.

From the trailhead at the end of the plowed County Road 10, ski or snowshoe up the Boreas Pass Road, the same route that was once used by the old South Park & Pacific Railroad trains. Immediately you'll notice that you have spectacular views of the Blue River Valley and the majestic Ten Mile Range mountains. The route continues for nearly 0.5 mile, and then you'll reach Rocky Point, where vistas of the entire Ten Mile Range will greet you. You'll be able to look down and see the city of Breckenridge and the downhill ski runs that are winding in and out of trees far to the west. For an altitude and "air check," you've climbed a total of about 200 feet higher than the trailhead.

After almost 1.5 miles on the trail, the route continues its gradual climb in and out of tree stands and then makes a big twist, first to the left and then the right. Entering a clearing you'll see a trail that cuts off to the north. Continue on the main trail, the wide one that follows along the railroad bed, weaving through trees and climbing gradually. Most of the route is gradual, but there are a couple of areas where the trail climbs on about an 8 percent to 11 percent grade. At about the 3.5-mile point, the route will curve to the left and drop you into an open meadow, where there was once an old mining settlement. A few of the old structures should be visible through the snow.

Just ahead, and before you cross a small creek, you'll see historic Baker's Tank. In days gone by the old steam-powered locomotives would stop here and take on additional water for their boilers from this lonesome tank and outpost before continuing their trek up and over the 11,481-foot Boreas Pass. This is a natural place to stop for a break, enjoy the views, have lunch, and then turn around if you're not planning on continuing up to the pass.

If you are looking for a more advanced workout and want to go all the way to the top of Boreas Pass, the route continues for another 3.6 miles past the Baker's Tank to the summit of Boreas Pass. From here and to the end, a large portion of this trail takes you above the timberline. Although the trail is easy to follow, the lack of trees can make for plenty of

Directions at a glance

- From the trailhead at the end of the plowed Boreas Pass Road, continue up the road that was once the railroad bed.

- At 0.5 mile you've reached Rocky Point—great views of town down below.

- At 1.5 miles from the trailhead, the trail continues a gentle climb and twists left and right ending up in a meadow. An old mining road cuts off on your left and to the north.

- Stay on main railroad bed to the 3.5-mile point, look out for mining settlement structures.

- Go another 0.25 mile to Baker's Tank. Good lunch spot or turn-around area.

- If continuing to the summit or the Section House, continue to follow the main trail. Two miles past Baker's Tank are remnants of old buildings that were once the town of Dyersville.

- After Dyersville you ski across open and gentle hillsides for next 1.6 miles with very little tree cover. At the summit, look for the Section House hut, it's easy to spot.

windy hiking or skiing. Check the weather forecasts and try to choose a clear and wind-calm day for this outing.

After you leave Baker's Tank, the trail continues for much the same over the next mile. At about the 2.0-mile point after Baker's Tank, you'll see a group of old buildings from Dyersville, and that's where you'll unfortunately leave the wind shelter and windbreak of the big trees. As you continue your now easy-to-moderate trail route, the last 1.5 miles or so brings you over open and gentle hillsides before the trail heads south. You'll steadily climb alongside or on the old railroad bed until it reaches the summit of Boreas Pass. You'll also best appreciate why this was the highest elevation, narrow-gauge railroad in the United States.

For the return trip you just go back the way you came, taking advantage of the gentle downward glide, just about all the way back to your vehicle.

If you are on a day trip and make it all the way to the Boreas Summit, the Summit Huts and Trails Association policy is that if you want to use the Section House to warm up before trekking back down the mountain, you must let the guests in residence know that you are there. You must also ask permission to come in and "warm up." Courteousness and respectfulness toward your hosts' privacy is always appreciated. The Section House offers solar-powered electricity, propane cooktops, firewood, and all the usual hut amenities. Water is obtained by melting snow, hence no dogs are allowed. The cost is $26 (plus tax) per person, per night.

How to get there

From Denver go west on I–70 and take exit 230 (Highway 9). Go south on Colorado Highway 9 for approximately 10.0 miles and enter the city of Breckenridge. At the southern end of the town, turn left onto Boreas Pass Road (County Road 10). There will be a large sign explaining the history of Boreas Pass, located a short distance up the road. It makes interesting reading if you have the time to stop and digest it. If not, continue approximately 3.5 miles up County Road 10, as it winds through Illinois Gulch. After traveling about 1.0 mile, County Road bends into a sharp hairpin turn to the left. Then the road makes a long and gentle turn back to the right and ends at the trailhead. This is at the end of the plowed road.

Peaks Trail

Breckenridge, CO

Type of trail:	▬▬▬ ⊛
Distance:	10 miles one way, return shuttle service available
Terrain:	Flat with gentle climbs and fun descent at end of trail into the town of Frisco.
Trail difficulty:	Advanced beginner to intermediate
Surface quality:	Ungroomed but usually well tracked by skiers/shoers.
Elevation:	Trailhead at Breckenridge 10,250 feet, highest point 10,400 feet; trail ends at 9,561 feet in Frisco
Time:	3 to 6 hours
Avalanche danger:	Low
Food and facilities:	Trail supplies—trail lunches, snacks, and water—can be found in Breckenridge and Frisco, depending on which way you plan to trek or ski the route. Both towns offer great dining for lunch and dinner, warm-up coffee or hot chocolate, and plenty of places for lounging, sightseeing, and shopping. For shuttle information, routes, and times from Frisco to Breckenridge, call the Summit Stage folks at (970) 668-0999.

Peaks Trail is fun and very popular because it links the two Colorado mountain towns of Breckenridge and Frisco in a 10-mile stretch for cross-country skiers and snowshoers. Although the trail can be done from both directions, the most popular route is to begin in Breckenridge and finish in Frisco. Even though the mileage distance seems a little long for the advanced beginner or intermediate snowshoer/skier, the route is generally very flat and has some nice downhill trekking or skiing runs.

It's also a very popular route for many winter users who don't want to partake in a full day of skiing or snowshoeing. Whenever they feel they've had enough of a workout, they are able to return to the trailhead at Breckenridge. If you want to trek or ski all the way from one town to the other, you can always drive from one town or the other (10 miles on Highway 9) and leave a shuttle car parked.

Of if you'd rather, *free* shuttle bus transportation between Breckenridge and Frisco or Frisco and Breckenridge—getting from one town to the other—usually isn't much of a problem. At either site are no-charge municipal shuttle buses that will pick you up and take you back to the general vicinity of your vehicle. Be sure to check with the Summit Stage

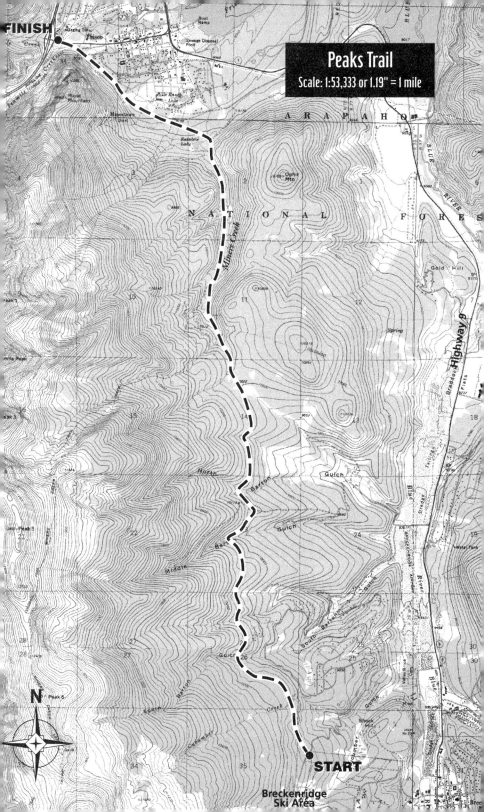

folks locally about schedules and routes—times and exact pickup and drop-off points vary throughout the season.

The easiest and most popular route is to start in Breckenridge and head toward Frisco only because the trail is very flat for the majority of the route and ends with a nice-to-moderate descent downhill into the town of Frisco. After a long day of skiing, gliding, or shoe trekking, a good and final downhill run can be most welcoming!

Designed specifically for cross-country skiers and cross-country showshoers, this is a trail that is well marked all the way with blue diamonds or red flagging tape and is a pleasure for beginners as well as skiers/shoers with more experience. The meadowlike clearings will provide you with some great opportunities to rest and take in the breathtaking views of the almost 14,000-foot peaks that surround the trail.

Regular users and visitors say that this is one of Colorado's best trails. First-timers love it because it's easy and never too crowded; beginners don't have to worry about competing for trail space with snowmobilers. On this 10.0-mile stretch snowmobiles are strictly prohibited, which makes the trail very peaceful and secluded. In addition because most of it is down in the treeline area, it's sheltered from the wind and gives the user the true feeling of a gentle stroll through the woods.

From the Breckenridge trailhead the first part of the route follows along and traverses the lower portions of the Ten Mile Range, weaving into and out of thick glades of trees.

Directions at a glance

- From the Breckenridge trailhead, the first 0.5 mile gently weaves through trees.
- Cross Cucumber Creek.
- Descend into clearing cut by U.S. Forest Service.
- At junction in Middle Barton Gulch, take left fork of trail.
- Follow trail north for several miles, passing North Barton Gulch and leaving tree cover for open meadows.
- For the last few miles the trail heads northwest along creek bed and then descends along Miners Creek.
- Stay on trail and pass the sign to Rainbow Lake.
- At T intersection (0.25 miles past Rainbow Lake cutoff) turn left on plowed road.
- Ski, trek, or board about 0.5 mile until road intersects Highway 9.
- Find shuttle bus pickup point and enjoy free ride back to Breckenridge.

It's fairly wide and level with only a moderate climb before crossing Cucumber Creek. After the creek, about 0.5 mile from the trailhead, you will continue to ski or snowshoe north until descending into a clearing. The U.S. Forest Service harvested the trees and created this small meadow within the last few years to open it up for improved wildlife habitat and to improve the health of the forest by creating age and size differences among all of the trees. The short-term benefit for you is that it's provided several cross-country "play" areas.

You will next come to a junction in the Middle Barton Gulch area. Take the left fork, staying on a well-established trail. Following the trail north for another couple of miles, you'll pass North Barton Gulch and leave the shelter of the trees, again skiing into some open meadows.

The last few miles the trail heads northwest along a creek bed, descending along Miners Creek and then into the town of Frisco. Here is where you can take off that hiking gear and strap on a snowboard for a ride down the hill. During the cold winter, and especially after a real frigid night of below-freezing or even below zero temperatures, this last part of the trail route can get "fast and icy." Out of the entire journey, it's only the last couple of icy downhill miles that gives this route its intermediate rating.

While skiing into and along the Miners Creek Valley, stay on the road toward the north and gently downhill and meander into and out of the woods. Pass the sign to Rainbow Lake and stay on the main road. After you've passed the sign to Rainbow Lake, within 0.25 mile, you'll hit a T intersection—it's a plowed road. Make a left at the "T" and head west for about 0.50 mile until you reach Highway 9 in Frisco.

You can then walk to where you parked your shuttle vehicle at the west end of Frisco or simply look for the numerous signed shuttle bus stops along the route. A bus will pick you up and transport you back to the Breckenridge area.

How to get there

Take the Frisco/Breckenridge exit (203) off I–70 and drive approximately 10 miles south on Highway 9, which takes you to Breckenridge and the downtown area. Come to the stop light in the middle of the town and make a right, turning west on Ski Hill Road (or County Road 3). Continue on CR 3 and drive past the Peak 8 Ski Area for about another 0.5 mile. You'll come to a plowed area on the left side of the road that is marked with a Peaks Trail trailhead sign.

French Gulch

Breckenridge, CO

Type of trail:	▬▬▬ ⬤⬤⬤
Distance:	6.2 miles
Terrain:	Flat with gentle climbs along road bed.
Trail difficulty:	Easy
Surface quality:	Ungroomed but usually well tracked by skiers/shoers.
Elevation:	Trailhead at 10,396 feet, climbs to 11,003 feet
Time:	2 to 4 hours
Avalanche danger:	Low
Food and facilities:	Located so close to Breckenridge there are plenty of lodging options and places to eat and get daytime supplies. Rentals, repairs, and backcountry supplies are available through the Breckenridge Nordic Ski Center (970–453–6855) or from Mountain Outfitters (970–453–2201).

The French Gulch area is a fun snowshoeing and skiing area because it abounds with history. In 1860 a miner named French Pete discovered gold here, luring hoards of hardrock miners to scour the hillsides, searching for their treasures. Although there were many more busts than booms, the area became a bonanza for gold, silver, zinc, and lead. On July 23, 1887, the largest gold nugget ever found in Colorado was discovered in French Gulch. Nicknamed "Tom's Baby," it was discovered by Tom Groves and a friend, Harry Lytton, who stumbled upon the whopping thirteen-pound chunk on Farncomb Hill.

The intact remnants of the mines, along with rounded piles of tailings left by dredging operations, are still strewn over the area, paying silent homage to the area's literally rich gold country history. There are also signs along the trails that explain the various mining techniques used in days gone by. Most of the dilapidated structures are found on private lands and can be very dangerous. Don't go exploring. Not only are you likely to be trespassing, but you could also become injured.

After parking around the Lincoln area where the snowplowed road ends, ski, shoe, or just hike and carry your gear over to the French Gulch roadbed. This roadbed is flat and fairly wide, so if you are a beginning skier or snowshoer and just want to visit the area and take in the scenery rather than have a strenuous cross-country workout in the backcountry, this area is ideal for you. A couple of hundred yards from the trailhead,

French Gulch

Scale: 1:24,000 or 2.64" = 1 mile

START

FINISH

N

the road will cut to the south and then head west toward the Sally Barber Mine. Leave the road and stay on the trail that goes straight, heading east. The trail will traverse alongside Humbug Hill, with spectacular views of Mount Guyot visible to the south. The climb remains steady but gentle. Between the 1.0- and 2.0-mile mark, you'll climb gently at a rate of about 105 feet per mile. As you continue to trek alongside the creek at the bottom of French Gulch, you will pass several privately owned cabins. The hill to your north is Farncomb Hill, where the thirteen-pound monster gold nugget was discovered!

Continue southeast on a gently rolling run between mile 2 and 3 and expect an altitude increase of about 300 feet. As you ski or shoe along, take this great opportunity to enjoy the breathtaking vistas of Bald Mountain. In total you've ascended some 1,000 feet and descended about 600 feet. The nice thing is that the climbs and descents are so gradual, and you're going to welcome the opportunity to point your shoes or skis back down the hill and enjoy the gradual glide or hike back to the trailhead.

> ## Directions at a glance
>
> - From the end of the plowed road, climb, ski, or shoe to the French Gulch roadbed.
> - Road continues to cut to the south a couple of hundred yards from the trailhead.
> - Ignore the road that cuts off or goes west. Go straight.
> - Traverse the sides of Humbug and Farncomb Hills for 2.0 miles.
> - Keep French Gulch and French Creek on your right side
> - Follow trail to end and then return.

When you're really ready to give up the spectacular views and scenery and come back, just turn around and follow the same route back to the trailhead.

How to get there

From I-70 take the Frisco/Breckenridge exit (203) and drive 9.3 miles south on Highway 9. Make a left turn onto County Road 450. Watch carefully because it is marked only with a street sign and can be easily missed. Follow CR 450 through a housing subdivision. After the development, CR 450 runs straight and then turns into County Road 2. Total driving distance from Highway 9 to the trailhead at Lincoln is approximately 4.1 miles.

If you miss the left turn onto County Road 450, continue on into the city of Breckenridge and turn left, or east, on Wellington Road (one block north of Ski Hill Road/Lincoln Avenue). Continue on Wellington as it curves left out of town to French Gulch. At the intersection with County Road 450, turn right. County Road 450 will turn into County Road 2. Continue to a parking area at the end of the plowed road, about 3.9 miles from Highway 9.

Parking space is limited so please do not parallel park on county roads or in private drives. A lot of the land along the trail is privately owned, so respect the private property by staying on the marked trail.

Photo by Tari and Andy Lightbody

Burro Trail

Breckenridge, CO

Type of trail:	▬▬ 🐾
Also used by:	Area before trail is used by skiers and snowmobilers at the Breckenridge Ski Resort area.
Distance:	6.2 miles to and from Burro Trail; 8.2 miles to and from Spruce Creek Road trailhead.
Terrain:	Moderate climb at beginning and then gentle climbs to trail end.
Trail difficulty:	Easy to intermediate
Surface quality:	Ungroomed but usually well tracked by skiers/shoers.
Elevation:	Trailhead at the Beaver Run ski lift is 9,746, goes to 10,600 at Spruce Creek Road
Time:	3 to 4 hours
Avalanche danger:	Low
Food and facilities:	No facilities for food, water, or rest rooms are found on the trail. The starting and stopping areas center around the Breckenridge Ski Resort area, which provides plenty of food, restaurant, and lodging opportunities. On the inbound journey, most restaurant and lounge facilities are open until late afternoon/early evening. For closest accommodations the Great Divide Hotel at Breckenridge (970–453–4500) is located just across the road from the trailhead. Accommodations are deluxe, but reasonably priced for overnight stays.

Rental gear for cross-country skiing and snowshoeing is available through the Breckenridge Nordic Ski Center (970–453–6855) or through Mountain Outfitters (970–453–2201).

The Burro Trail is enjoyable and easy for skiers or snowshoers at any level. It's sheltered by trees, climbs with only a gradual ascent, and does not permit snowmobiles to interrupt your peaceful and easy journey. As you ski or snowshoe along, catch glimpses of Mount Baldy and the Boreas Pass Trail to the east. It's private and quiet here, and yet so close to the Breckenridge ski lifts that it's a great, convenient outing if you're a downhill skier who wants something different or a visitor who has never cross-country skied before.

If you're staying at one of the hotel resorts on the mountain, the trail is within easy walking distance. The Great Divide Hotel at Breckenridge

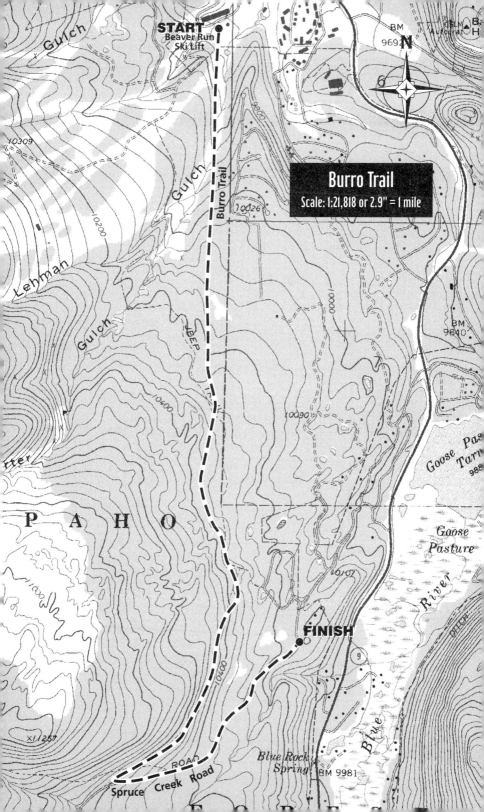

is literally just across the road from the trailhead and is less than a five-minute walk to the base of the Beaver Run lift. Rental equipment is available through either the Breckenridge Nordic Ski Center or through Mountain Outfitters.

The first part of the trail, starting at the Burro Trail/Peak 9 trailhead, is a little narrow, and it climbs. If you're a beginner and don't want to tackle the ascent, you might want to choose the more open, meadow areas of the Lower Lehman Ski Run at the base of the mountain. You'll be a little west of the Burrow Trail, so just head south and intersect the trail at about the 0.5-mile point, or whenever you feel comfortable.

The Burro Trail doesn't have any sharp curves and meanders through forests of lodgepole pines, spruce, and fir trees. At just over 1.5 miles from the trailhead, the route starts bending to the right or southwest. The Burro Trail intersects an old four-wheel-drive vehicle trail and continues a gentle climb or ascent. You'll continue in this direction for another 1.0 mile until the end of Burro Trail, where it intersects Spruce Creek Road. At this point you have the choice of turning around and heading back to the Peak 9 area or heading up or down the Spruce Creek Road Trail. (It's a road in the summer and a trail in the winter.)

If you decide to turn around, you'll get the benefit of a nice and gentle, very gradual glide back down the trail. If you're a beginning skier, however, remember that the last 0.5 mile leading back into the Peak 9/Burro trailhead will be narrow and a little fast.

Directions at a glance

- Head to the base of the Beaver Run at the Breckenridge Ski Resort.
- Ski across the base of the downhill run south to the trailhead of the Burro Trail/Peak 9 Trail.
- Follow the trail signs straight up the hill.
- (Option: If you don't want to do the moderate climb, stay west of the trail through the Lehman Ski Run. It's a more open meadow and gentler climb.)
- At just over 1.5 miles, the trail bends slightly right to the southwest and intersects an old 4x4 vehicle trail.
- Trail continues with a gentle climb.
- Follow trail for another 1.0 mile where Burro Trail intersects Spruce Creek Road.
- Turn around and enjoy a gentle downhill return back to ski resort or make sharp left turn (east) and continue up Spruce Creek Road Trail.
- If you're planning a one-way trip, pick up your shuttle vehicle at the Spruce Creek Road trailhead. If not, turn and hike back to the Burro Trail and enjoy the downhill glide back to the Breckenridge Ski Resort.

If you left your shuttle vehicle at the Spruce Creek trailhead, follow Spruce Creek Road, which veers sharply to the left, or east. It's a gentle downhill glide or hike as you head east for 0.25 mile or so, following the trickling waters of Spruce Creek. Then it starts to track northeast. In less than 1.0 mile you'll reach the trailhead, at which point you can turn back around and do it all over again, or, if you parked your car at this end of the route, call it a day and head back to the Great Divide Hotel for some great food, drink, and a soak in their indoor hot tubs!

How to get there

From Denver take I–70 west to the Frisco/Breckenridge exit (203). Go south from exit 203 on Highway 9 and travel about 10.0 miles to downtown Breckenridge. From the downtown Breckenridge parking areas, you can take the free Breckenridge shuttle buses to the base of the Beaver Run Ski Lift area. Ski about 100 yards across the ski run to the Burro Trail/Peak 9 trailhead on the south side of the run. Look for the signs, it is well marked.

If you want to ski only one way and then drive back into town, you can leave a shuttle car at the Spruce Creek trailhead. From downtown Breckenridge, drive south on Highway 9 for approximately 2.0 miles to the Spruce Creek Road (CR 800). Make a right and head west on the road for about 0.5 to 0.75 mile until you reach the end of the plowed road. Use the Spruce Creek trailhead area for parking.

Mohawk Lake

Breckenridge, CO

Type of trail:	▬▬▬ ⬤
Also used by:	Snowmobilers
Distance:	6.6 miles
Terrain:	Easy beginning and then steady and moderate climbs all the way to lake. Great downhill run back to the trailhead.
Trail difficulty:	Intermediate to advanced
Surface quality:	Ungroomed but often well tracked by skiers/shoers.
Elevation:	Trailhead is 10,200 feet, climbs to 12,100 feet; elevation change is 1,954 feet
Time:	3 to 5 hours
Avalanche danger:	Low to high
Snowmobile use:	Low
Food and facilities:	No facilities are found along the trail. Because of the close proximity to the city of Breckenridge, there are plenty of places to gas up your vehicle, purchase sack lunches and snacks, and rent either cross-country skiing or snowshoeing equipment. Breckenridge Nordic Ski Center (970–453–8855) or Mountain Outfitters (970–453–2201) can handle just about all your equipment needs and repairs. The Great Divide Hotel in Breckenridge (970–453–4500) is centrally located in the town and has great guest services representatives who cater to the winter outdoor enthusiasts.

A favorite among the locals of Breckenridge—and soon to be a favorite for readers of this book—the Mohawk Lake Trail offers spectacular views of the surrounding peaks, the wooded areas of the Arapaho National Forest, and of mining areas of days gone by. It also offers a choice of deep powder snow areas that are tempting to the cross-country skier, the snowboarder, and the snowshoer.

It's a steady, gradual, and constant climb from the Spruce Creek trailhead to the Mohawk Lake area. The climb is not suggested for even intermediate skiers or shoers unless they are in good physical condition. The trip up the hills involves nearly a 2,000-foot altitude increase in just over 3.0 miles. However, on the return, it provides you with great downhill trekking and skiing back to the trailhead. If you are an intermediate and advanced winter enthusiast, all of this awaits you less than 20 minutes from the Breckenridge Ski Resort and all of the city amenities.

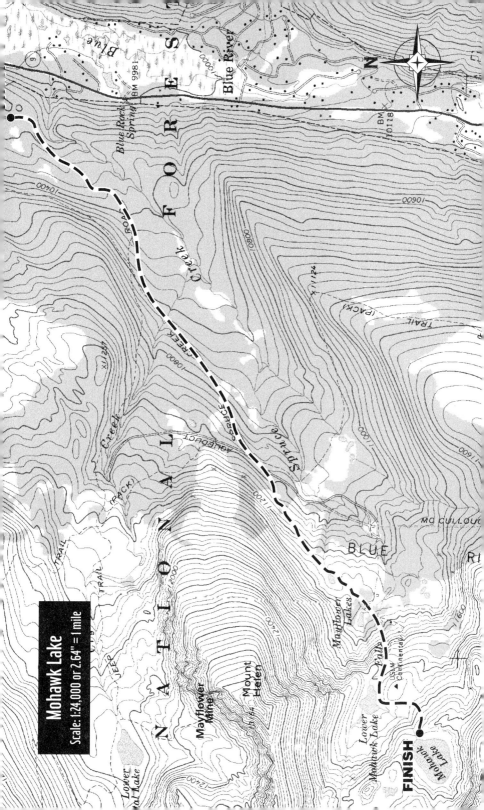

Mohawk Lake

Scale: 1:24,000 or 2.64" = 1 mile

FINISH

From the trailhead head southwest on Spruce Creek Road and ski into a forest thick with conifers. Almost immediately to the southwest, the 13,950-foot Pacific Peak greets you. At a little less than 0.5 mile, you'll ski along a switchback and see a marker to the right for the turnoff to Burro Trail. Keep going southwest along the Spruce Creek Road Trail, climbing out of the trees and into the open. Just after the 1.3-mile point, you'll come across the junction for the Wheeler Trail. The Aqueduct Road cuts back to the north, or on your right at this junction, and would lead you to Francie's Cabin (see "Francie's Cabin Trail," page 112), and the Lower and Upper Crystal Lakes Trail. The trail to the left, or south, is a continuation of the Wheeler Trail that goes another 3.5 miles and comes back out to join Highway 9.

You access the trail to Mohawk Lake by continuing southwest on the Spruce Creek Road Trail until you get to an open clearing at the end of the road. Depending on the time of year and snow conditions, there could be avalanche danger in the area. Check with the Avalanche Control Center at (970) 668–0600. If the danger is above the "low" level, you are advised to leave the road area and descend closer to the creek for safety sake.

To the north of this area is the historic Mayflower Mine, discovered in 1887. In its "prime" or "golden days," the mine yielded outstanding ore, bearing 30 ounces of gold per ton. Much evidence of the mining activity in the late 1800s and early 1900s still exists. On the trail you'll see remnants from an old mill and a huge wheel that was used to generate waterpower. Several mining companies struck claims in the mountains, burrowing tunnels as much as 800 feet into the rocks—all in search of large veins of gold and the Mother Lode.

At the end of Spruce Creek Road, you'll look for the trail that leads to Mayflower Lakes. After a 0.25-mile uphill trek to the west, the trail makes a hard left turn to the southwest. Another 0.25 mile and you've arrived at Mohawk Lake. At Mohawk Lake take a breather and enjoy the vistas of 13,164-foot Mount Helen and the Ten-Mile Range.

Directions at a glance

- From the trailhead travel southwest on Spruce Creek Road for 1.3 miles.

- At the junction the trail to north (right) leads to Francie's Cabin, and trail to south (left) heads off on the Wheeler Trail. Don't take either one!

- Stay on Spruce Creek Road Trail until it ends in a meadow. Look for the trail sign to Mayflower Lakes.

- Follow the trail 0.25 mile uphill to the west. Then make a hard turn left to the southwest. One-quarter mile more and you will arrive at Mohawk Lake.

Photo by Biege Jones, courtesy of Aspen Skiing Company

To return to the trailhead just follow the trail back, enjoy an almost 2,000-foot descent for great downhill snowshoeing or skiing.

How to get there

Take the Frisco/Breckenridge exit (203) off of I–70 and drive approximately 10.0 miles south on Highway 9. This will take you into the middle of Breckenridge. From downtown Breckenridge take Highway 9 south for approximately 2.0 miles, then turn right on Spruce Creek Road (CR 800). Head west on Spruce Creek Road for about 0.5 to 0.75 mile, until you reach the end of the plowed road. Use the Spruce Creek trailhead area for parking.

Francie's Cabin

Breckenridge, CO

Type of trail:	▬▬ ●
Distance:	Easiest route to and from the Cabin—6 miles
	More difficult route to and from the Cabin—4.2 mile
	Easiest route to and from Lake—8.2 miles
	More difficult route to and from the Lake—6.4 miles
Terrain:	Easy beginning and then steady and moderate climbs to the Cabin and then the Lake.
Trail difficulty:	Intermediate to difficult
Surface quality:	Ungroomed but often well tracked by skiers/shoers.
Elevation:	Trailhead is at 10,180 feet; hut is at 11,300 feet.
Time:	3 to 5 hours
Avalanche danger:	Low
Food and facilities:	No facilities are available on the trail. Load up with food, snacks, and water before leaving Breckenridge. The trail is only a couple miles south of town. If you're packing into Francie's Cabin for an overnight stay, make sure to bring groceries. The cabin has beds, firewood, lanterns, propane cooking, and utensils. Make sure you bring your own sleeping bag. Reservations for the cabin must be made in advance. Call the Tenth Mountain Hut Association at (970) 925–5775.

Francie's Cabin is one of three huts built by the Summit County Huts and Trails Association. It has quickly become a popular destination because of its proximity to Spruce and Crystal Creeks in wonderful backcountry areas for ski touring and snowshoeing. There are two ways to get there: either use the Spruce Creek Road or the Crystal Creek Trail. If you want a relatively easy trip from the trailhead, take Spruce Creek Road. It's a gentle road that was built for summer travel; it's easy to follow, fast, and takes you right to the cabin.

If you feel a little wild and want the challenge of a good stiff climb on the inbound route or steep descents on the outbound leg of the trip, take the Crystal Creek Trail. With an elevation change of over 750 feet in just 1.0 mile, this old four-wheel-drive road gives the skier plenty of thrills . . . or spills. Climbing skins are a must, and the route may be better suited for snowshoers who don't have gravity working against them.

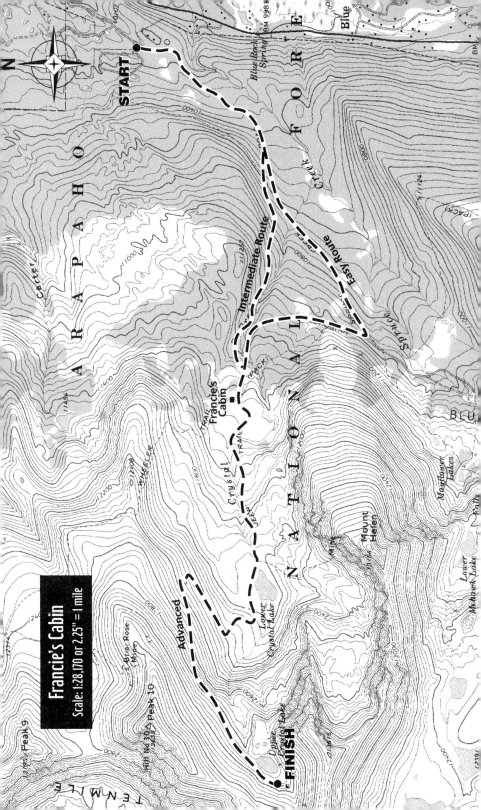

Francie's Cabin
Scale: 1:28,170 or 2.25" = 1 mile

START

FINISH

Easy Route

Intermediate Route

Advanced

Francie's Cabin

ARAPAHO

FOREST

NATIONAL

Blue

Blue Rocks
Springs

Creek

Spruce

Crystal

Lower
Crystal Lake

Upper
Crystal Lake

Mount
Helen

Mayflower
Lakes

Lower
Mohawk Lake

Wheeler

Peak 9

Peak 10

Gold Rose
Mine

TENMILE

BLU

To access both the routes, begin skiing or snowshoeing southwest along Spruce Creek Road. It does not allow any snowmobile traffic and has been posted. The road climbs gradually and will intersect the Crystal Creek Trail at about a 1.0 mile from the trailhead. If you decide to take on the challenge of a hard climb that includes elevation grades of from 9 to 24 percent increase in grades, head west on Crystal Creek Trail and go for it. You'll go approximately 1.3 miles and intersect with the Wheeler Trail right before you reach Francie's Cabin.

If you decide on the gentler route, stay on Spruce Creek Road for another 1.0 mile, heading southwest. At that point, you'll see an aqueduct road running north and south. Take that road toward the north. It will gradually bend around to the northwest and meet up with the Wheeler Trail. Blue diamond signs will show you the way to the cabin.

Directions at a glance

- From the trailhead go southwest 1.0 mile on Spruce Creek Road.
- At the 1.0-mile point, look for cutoff to the west. This is the Crystal Creek Trail.
- For the easiest route stay on Spruce Creek Road another 1.0 mile, heading southwest.
- Two miles from the trailhead, you'll see Aqueduct Road cutting off on your right and to the north.
- Take the Aqueduct Road north for approximately 0.75 mile. Where it meets the Wheeler Trail, look for blue diamonds that will lead you to Francie's Cabin.

Alternate route

- From the trailhead go southwest 1.0 mile on Spruce Creek Road.
- At approximately 1.0 mile, look for the Crystal Creek Trail, which cuts off on your right to the west.
- If you take this more advanced trail, plan on some steeper climbing.
- When it crosses the Wheeler Trail, look for blue diamonds that will lead you to the cabin.

If you don't have reservations to stay at the cabin and want to further explore the area, keep going on Crystal Creek Trail west for about 1.0 mile, and you'll come upon Lower Crystal Lake. There you'll find the remnants of a silver mining operation that dates back to the late 1800s and early 1900s. A magnificent view of Mount Helen, which stretches 13,164 feet into the sky, can be seen to the south. This area was also once heavily mined and yielded a lot of lead-based ores. It now yields spectacular views of craggy peaks.

If you want to press on, you can continue to ski or snowshoe on the four-wheel-drive Crystal Creek Trail. To reach the end of the trail, it's just under 2.0 miles, but it has elevation grades of from 8 percent to 23 percent and is recommended for those who are advanced skiers/shoers and in very good physical condition. You'll bend around a minor switchback, head northeast, and then veer west around the south side of Peak 10 of the Breckenridge Ski Resort. Another turn toward the southwest and you'll arrive at Upper Crystal Lake with an elevation of 12,850 feet.

If you are making a day trip and want to stop and rest around Francie's Cabin, please respect the privacy of the guests staying there. Dogs are not allowed because the water for the cabin is obtained by melting snow that's retrieved from outside. Overnight stays are $26 (plus tax) per person and include all the basic amenities—beds, firewood, cooking supplies, etc.

On your return you can retrace the route down Spring Creek Road for the mild tour, or go down the Crystal Lakes 4x4 trail for a wild descent!

How to get there

Take I–70 west from Denver to the Frisco/Breckenridge exit (203). From exit 203 go south on Highway 9 approximately 10.0 miles to downtown Breckenridge. From downtown Breckenridge drive south on Highway 9 for approximately 2.0 miles to Spruce Creek Road (CR 800). Good signage will direct you to make a right turn at the turnoff. Head west on Spruce Creek Road for about 0.5 to 0.75 mile, until you reach the end of the plowed road. Use the Spruce Creek trailhead area for parking.

Janet's Cabin

Copper Mountain Ski Resort

Type of trail:	▬▬▬ ⊕⊕
Also used by:	First portion—0.25 mile—used by downhill skiers at Copper Mountain Ski Resort.
Distance:	9.2 miles to and from Union Creek trailhead; or 7.6 miles when taking ski lift to the mountaintop
Terrain:	Steady and gentle climbs to the Cabin and easy glide/trek downhill back to the trailhead.
Trail difficulty:	Advanced beginner/intermediate
Surface quality:	Ungroomed but usually well tracked by skiers/shoers.
Elevation:	Union Creek trailhead at 9,820 feet; Janet's Cabin at 11,610 feet
Time:	3 to 5 hours
Avalanche danger:	Low
Food and facilities:	Cross-country and snowshoe rentals, lodging, restaurants, a convenience store, rest rooms, and repair shop are all available at the Copper Mountain Ski Resort (970) 968–2318. Guided tours to Janet's Cabin for both skiers and snowshoers are offered by the Copper Mountain Cross-Country Center. Call the resort number (extension 6342). Special 2-day, 1-night "gourmet packages" are also offered through the Cross Country Ski Center and can include guides and all meal preparations. For additional information or general reservations for use of Janet's Cabin, call the Tenth Mountain Hut Association (303–925–5775). Groceries for an extended stay are best picked up in the town of Frisco, which lies 8 miles to the east, just off of I–70.

Janet's Cabin is one of the area's most popular huts partly because its trailhead is conveniently located close to the metro areas of the Front Range at the Copper Mountain Ski Resort.

Nestled in the trees near the head of Guller Creek along the Colorado Trail, Janet's Cabin was built in 1990 and is a memorial to Janet Boyd Tyler, a Vail resident who was active in Colorado skiing for many years before she died of cancer in 1988. This area was also a favorite training ground for the Tenth Mountain Division, elite ski troops during World War II.

The trail invites skiers of all abilities because of its short and easy-to-follow route. It's ideal for day skiers who want the experience of back-

Janet's Cabin

Scale: 1:34,286 or 1.85" = 1 mile

Copper Mountain Ski Resort

START

Alternate Route

Main Route Ride Ski Lift

Union Mountain

Union Gulch

Copper Mountain

Wheeler

Jacque Creek

Jacque Ridge

Guller Creek

Searle

Janet's Cabin

FINISH

country skiing without having to stay overnight in the hut. Day trips along this trail are often what skiers and snowshoers opt for, so the trail can sometimes be crowded.

For telemark skiers, snowboarders, or industrious snowshoers, there are incredible bowls above the cabin near Searle Pass and Sugarloaf Mountain ideal for carving turns or exploring. Like many trails in the area, the region is popular with snowboarders looking for open, uncrowded, and unused deep powder areas. Many shoers trekking into the area are often armed with a backpack that includes not only day supplies but a snowboard as well!

The cabin itself is a 2,700-square-foot log structure that offers a propane stove and burners, photovoltaic system for lighting, indoor

Directions at a glance

- At the Copper Mountain Ski Resort, take the K or L ski lift to the mountaintop.
- Ski less than 0.25 mile down the Ten Mile ski slope, then look for access gate on left to national forest.
- Ski downhill on Elk Track Trail to junction of Colorado Trail at Guller Creek.
- Ski southwest on Colorado Trail following Guller Creek for just over 2.6 miles.
- Climb steep hill (500 vertical feet) to cabin in last 0.25 mile.
- To return, follow the same route back down Guller Creek. Climb the hill out of Creek at the Ski Resort by going east. It will bring you out behind the Resort's Nordic Center and parking lot.

Alternate route (for day skiers or snowshoers)

- Go west on trail from Cross-Country Center at the Copper Mountain Ski Resort.
- Intersect the Colorado Trail at Guller Creek and go left.
- Ski the Colorado Trail along Guller Creek for approximately 3.7 miles.
- Climb steep hill (500 vertical feet) to cabin in last 0.25 mile.
- To return—follow the same route back down Guller Creek. Climb the hill out of Creek at the Ski Resort by going east. It will bring you out behind the Resort's Nordic Center and parking lot.

odorless toilets, a detached sauna, and cooking facilities, including utensils. The large facilities are rustic but very nicely appointed. Janet's Cabin has four bedrooms and can sleep up to twenty overnight guests.

If you are an overnight guest with reservations, you'll be issued a ride pass that's good for a one-way trip up either the K or L lift. From the base of the ski lift, simply board the lift for a short ride to the top of the mountain. From there follow the signs down the west edge of the "beginner" trail of the West Ten Mile run. You'll soon see the public access gate to the Arapaho National Forest. At the forest access, you'll ski down Elk Track Trail, a mostly gentle route with only a few steep descents through the conifers. Soon you'll meet the Colorado Trail/Guller Creek Trail and follow that for about 2.0 miles, skiing through meadows and forests, moderately gaining elevation. Just before the 3.0-mile point, you'll cross over a meadow and ski/shoe another 0.6 mile southwest. At about 0.25 mile from Janet's Cabin, you'll encounter a steep hill where you'll climb 500 feet in elevation to reach the hut. It's the last 0.5 mile where the terrain becomes steep climbing that gives this route its advanced beginner to intermediate rating.

If you're day skiing or snowshoeing only, free ski lift passes are obviously not provided, and you'll have to take the longer 5.0-mile route. From the Cross-Country Center at Copper Mountain, the trail starts on the side of the building. Hike or ski to the west end of the ski area and look for the public access sign. You'll be skiing or trekking across a downhill ski run, so watch for fast moving downhillers. Continue west until you intersect the Colorado Trail and then turn left. The trail follows along Guller Creek in a southwest direction. It's about 3.7 miles up the Colorado Trail and the climb is steady.

Please note that all of the Janet's Cabin facilities are *not* for use by day skiers, shoers, or snowboarders. Only skiers who are guests with reservations are allowed to use the cabin's rest rooms and other facilities and are asked to stay away from the cabin and respect the privacy of guests.

How to get there

From I–70 heading west out of Denver, take exit 195 (Highway 91) and go south less than 0.25 mile to the main entrance of the Copper Mountain Ski Resort. Turn west onto the resort road. Take the first left into the east parking lot and drive to the end of the lot. If you've made reservations for an overnight stay at Janet's Cabin, look for the designated overnight parking slots. Otherwise do not park in these spots—they are for guests with reservations only. Overnight guests should then proceed to the Cross-Country Center for final check-in and issuance of ski lift passes.

Wheeler Lakes

Copper Mountain Ski Resort

Type of trail:	━━━ ⬤
Distance:	4.0 miles
Terrain:	Steep and challenging climbs from the trailhead to Wheeler Lakes, with steep descents back to the trailhead.
Trail difficulty:	Advanced/expert
Surface quality:	Ungroomed backcountry conditions, and usually not well tracked by skiers/shoers.
Elevation:	Trail starts at about 9,700 feet, climbs to 11,100 feet; elevation changes nearly 1,300 feet.
Time:	3 to 5 hours
Avalanche danger:	Low
Food and facilities:	No food, water, or even rest rooms are available. Gas and a convenience store can be found just south of I–70 on Highway 91 for snacks, water, soft drinks, and ready-made sandwiches. Restaurant and lodging can also be found just south of I–70 on Highway 91 at the Copper Mountain Ski Resort (970–968–2318). If you're looking for anything fancy, your best bet is to head back on I–70 east and stop in Frisco. It's a major town with fast foods, a large grocery store, fancy dining, and plenty of fine overnight accommodations.

The Wheeler Lakes Trail that takes summer and winter users up to the high, nearly 13,000-foot lakes is renowned for its difficulty—both in the demands it makes on stamina and physical conditioning and on a user's ability to navigate through deep snows with minimal navigational markings. It's a trail that should only be attempted by advanced or expert skiers/snowshoers. Elevation grades average 20 percent to 40 percent. There's even a couple just over 50 percent inclines to really help keep your heart pumping. Winter enthusiasts who use the trail on a regular basis call doing so "training to be an iron man or iron woman." If you are out of shape, not an expert skier or snowshoer, and don't possess excellent backcountry wood skills, the message is clear—don't even think about tackling this one!

The Wheeler Lakes Trail is also called the Gore Range Trail. It has an elevation ascent that is steep and steeper. The avalanche danger is rated as low, but the trail does climb just over 1,300 feet in less than 2.0 miles from the trailhead and quickly leaves civilization behind. In less than 0.5

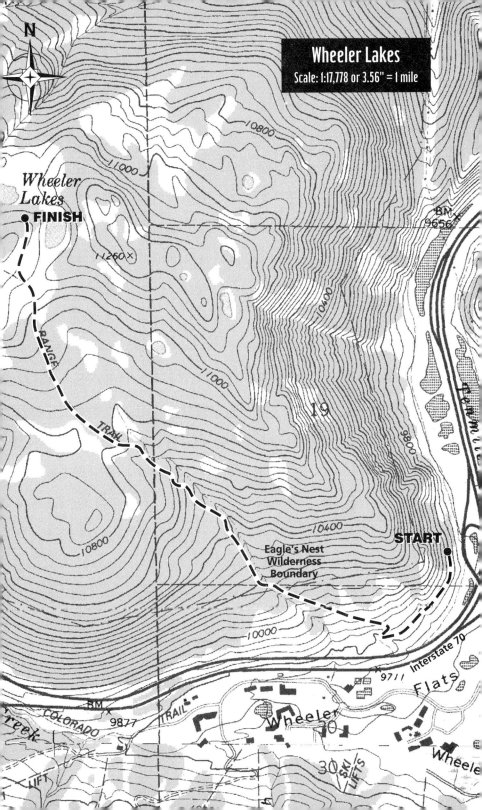

N

Wheeler Lakes
Scale: 1:17,778 or 3.56" = 1 mile

Wheeler
Lakes
● FINISH

10800

11000

11260 ×

RANGE

TRAIL

11000

10400

19

9800

BM ×
9656

Tenmile

10800

10400

START ●

Eagle's Nest
Wilderness
Boundary

10000

9711

Interstate 70

Flats

Wheeler

Wheele

BM ×
9877

COLORADO

TRAIL

20

Creek

LIFT

SKI
LIFTS

30

mile, you've entered the Eagle's Nest Wilderness Area, where no mechanized or motorized vehicle traffic is allowed. Unless you're on foot, skis, snowshoes, or horseback, you will not be allowed into the area. Often during the winter the deep snows completely cover and obliterate just about all of the trail markings. This means that the "designated trail/route" markings are extremely difficult to follow and sometimes even impossible to find! Excellent map-reading skills and compass knowledge are a must at minimum. Knowing how to read a map, match it to a compass, and then take reading from a global positioning satellite (GPS) receiver are your best bet for sure navigation.

In the summer months when the snows have melted, the Gore Range Trail to Wheeler Lakes is a popular and challenging route for campers seeking a hike-in wilderness experience. In the winter months you don't have to follow the summer trail. As we said earlier, chances are excellent that it's going to be hidden and often hard to find. However if you want to challenge yourself in this steep and deep terrain, the reward is phenomenal deep powder skiing and snowshoeing through meadows that peek out from the trees all along the steep hills and the trail. Inside the Eagle's Nest Wilderness Area, the remoteness and quiet are in stark contrast to the bustling sounds of the close-by Copper

Directions at a glance

- From the trailhead near Highway 91, go southwest approximately 0.2 miles through thick stands of aspen trees.

- Look for trailhead sign at this point and head northwest. Approximately 0.5 mile up the trail, look for Forest Service sign along trail, high above deep snow level. You've now reached the Eagle's Nest Wilderness Area.

- Trail turns northwest and continues its steep climb.

- When aspen trees turn to conifers, you've reached the halfway point.

- Trail veers more sharply north for next 0.5 mile and continues for just over another 0.5 mile.

- Look for intersection to Wheeler Lakes. Forest Service has posted wood sign here, and Wheeler Lakes is about 0.25 mile to the northeast.

- Take your time returning on the trail exactly as you came up.

Photo by Ben Blakenburg, courtesy of Copper Mountain Resort

Mountain Ski Resort and the always present heavy traffic on I–70, just a hairbreadth away to the south.

For your trek to the trailhead near Highway 91, go southwest approximately 0.2 mile through thick stands of aspen trees.

Look for trailhead sign at this point and head northwest, climbing through more thick groves of aspen trees. Approximately 0.5 mile up the trail, you'll see a wooden Forest Service sign posted high enough on a tree by the trail that it doesn't get buried by deep snows. It tells everyone that they're entering the Eagle's Nest Wilderness Area.

From here the trail starts turning in a more northwest direction. By the 1.0-mile point, you'll ascend 300 feet to the 10,000-foot elevation and see magnificent views of the Ten Mile Mountain Range to the east and the Vail Pass to the west. Below you to the south is the ski resort. As you continue north-northwest on the trail, you will climb steadily and begin to hike or ski in and out of dense glades of conifers. When the aspens give way to the evergreens, you know that you are near the halfway point to the lakes. If you have your altimeter or GPS receiver handy and feel like taking a reading, your elevation should be somewhere between 10,800 and 11,000 feet.

To reach Wheeler Lakes and complete the iron man/iron woman trek, continue in the same direction for about another 0.5 mile. The trail will then veer more sharply to the north over hilly meadows for another 0.5 mile. Keep a lookout for the intersection at the Gore Range Trail and Wheeler Lakes. Again it's marked by a Forest Service wood sign that should be nailed to a tree above the deep snow levels. If you don't find it, don't fret. The Wheeler Lakes are just ahead a little to the northeast, and you made it.

Return on the trail is exactly the same way you came up. Downhill snowshoe trekking or skiing may be less invigorating, but some spots are going to be steep and steeper. Take your time going up, and doubly take your time coming back down!

How to get there

Take I–70 west from Denver to Vail and then take exit 195 (Highway 91). Immediately on exiting from Interstate 70, you'll see the overpass off the designated off-ramp. Hit the brakes, slow down, and prepare yourself for some exacting directions. Don't cross over the I–70 overpass. Just before this point, you'll find the trailhead and the parking area north of the overpass, before you get onto Highway 91.

Look for a small dirt turnout area, and if there's room, park here. Unfortunately it only accommodates a couple of cars or one big truck. If there's no room to park, drive across the bridge (the overpass we've been telling you to avoid) and make a left into the Ten-Mile Canyon parking area and follow the signs back to the trailhead.

Mayflower Gulch

Copper Mountain Ski Resort

Type of trail:	▬▬ ⬤
Also used by:	Snowboarders
Distance:	3.4 miles
Terrain:	Moderate climbs to top of trail and then great deep powder bowls.
Trail difficulty:	Intermediate
Surface quality:	Ungroomed but sometimes tracked by skiers/shoers.
Elevation:	Trail starts at 10,905 feet and ends at 11,593 feet.
Time:	2 to 3 hours
Snowmobile use:	Minimal to none
Avalanche danger:	Low to moderate
Food and facilities:	None at the trailhead. Closest areas are the Copper Mountain Ski Resort, located 5 miles north on Highway 91, or the town of Leadville, which lies 17 miles to the south on Highway 91. At the Copper Mountain Ski Resort (970–968–2318), food and lodging are available. Advance reservations for lodging are strongly suggested. The resort's close proximity to the Mayflower Gulch Trail makes it an ideal place to stop and pick up snacks, a sack lunch, or a warming cup of coffee, either inbound or outbound.

Mayflower Gulch (also known as Mayflower Creek on some maps) is a favorite for locals who want to avoid the snowmobile traffic on Vail Pass, which is located farther to the north. Skiers often head to Boston Mine at the end of the 1.7-mile trail, ski in the deep powder on the bowls at the upper end of the valley, and then spend the night back at the Copper Mountain Ski Resort. Mayflower Gulch is also becoming a favorite for snowboarders. Using snowshoes to trek into the area, they pile up the hiking gear at the old Boston Mine and strap on snowboards for deep, virgin powder runs.

Whether you're skiing or shoeing, the route is usually well tracked and not difficult to follow. A few steep climbs give this trail its intermediate rating, and the total climbing required for the 1.7-mile trail inbound is around 760 vertical feet. The few small descents total only 71 feet.

From the Mayflower Gulch Creek trailhead, ski or snowshoe east on the road following the drainage for approximately 0.5 mile. The grade here is a maximum of 7 percent. At about the 0.5-mile point, you'll

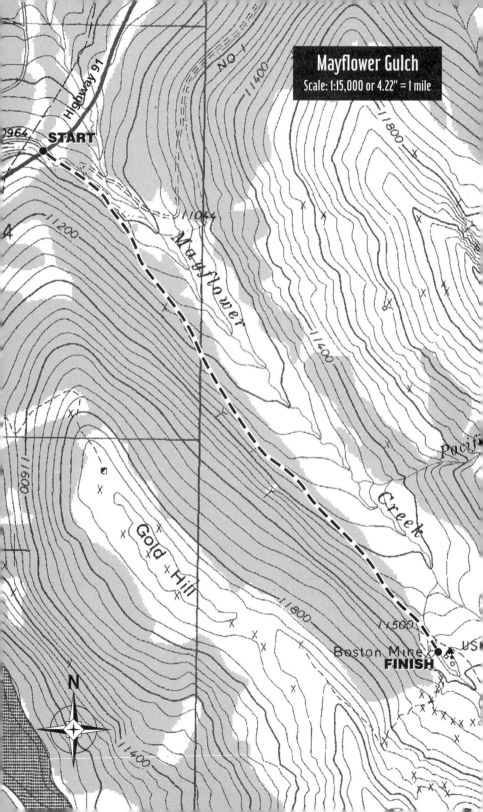

ascend a steep hill with a grade of about 17 percent. The trail bends to the southwest, zigzags, and finally heads southeast. At about the 1.0-mile point, you'll see a few small side roads that head off in all directions. These usually only go a couple of hundred yards and dead-end at mining test holes and piles of rock tailings. Continue southeast hiking upward—with one short ascent that is just over 23 percent incline—and then enter the valley of Mayflower Gulch. Keep the creek to the northwest or your left side and climb steadily into and out of glades of trees for the next 0.7 mile. After that you'll break out of the trees and see a group of old mining structures that once belonged to the Boston Mine. This is a great place to take pictures and rest before heading off to tackle one of the magnificent deep powder bowls.

To return to the trailhead, follow the same route you used to come in and enjoy the nearly constant downhill all the way back out of Mayflower Gulch.

How to get there

From Denver take I–70 west to exit 195 (Highway 91). Go south past the Copper Mountain Ski Resort and drive for 5.25 miles. Watch for road signs for Mayflower Creek. Just after Highway 91 crosses Mayflower Creek, look for a turnout on the right side of the road. Park off the road at the start of the gulch.

Directions at a glance

- From the trailhead, head east approximately 0.5 mile.
- Ascend hill and trail bends to southwest then zigzags southeast.
- At 1.0-mile point, numerous small side roads cut away from main trail.
- Continue on main trail southeast for about 0.7 mile.
- Look for remnants of the old Boston gold mine.
- To return, just follow the same route back to the trailhead.

Tennessee Pass Cookhouse (Dinner Yurt)

Cooper Hill Ski Area, Leadville, CO

Type of trail:	▬ ⬤ ◄
Also used by:	Snowmobilers
Distance:	2.0 miles
Terrain:	Easy climb up to the Cookhouse and gentle glide back down to the Ski Resort.
Trail difficulty:	Novice
Surface quality:	Groomed and always tracked by skiers/shoers.
Elevation:	Trail starts at 10,537 feet and climbs to 10,797 at the Cookhouse.
Time:	30 minutes
Food and facilities:	Because it's such a short "fun-run" to the Cookhouse, few if any advance preparations are going to be required. If you're going to stay in Vail and come 30 miles south for the dinner trek, it's advised that you make advance reservations for accommodations in the Vail area. You can get brochure information on all overnight facilities by calling the Vail/Beaver Creek Reservations at (800) 525–2257. Vail also has a host of grocery stores, convenience stores, gas stations, and top restaurants to select from.

A more moderately priced option to Vail is a stay in Leadville, located less than 10 miles south from the Tennessee Pass trailhead. Hotel, motel, and bed-and-breakfast information is available by calling the Leadville Chamber of Commerce at (719) 486–3900.

The Tennessee Pass Cookhouse can accommodate about thirty guests per evening. Package price of $50 per person also includes all your cross-country ski or snowshoe equipment, guides, headlamps, and dinner. Taxes, gratuities, and your bar tab are extra. For further information or reservations (which are a must!) call (719) 486–1750 or –8114.

This is not our usual backcountry trail since Bill's Trail starts at the Piney Creek Nordic Center and has really only one purpose—to take skiers and snowshoers to the Tennessee Pass Cookhouse. What makes this destination so unique is that it is the only gourmet restaurant in Colorado that's a yurt tucked back in the forest! Adhering to the U.S. Forest Service Code, which stipulates that structures in this area can only

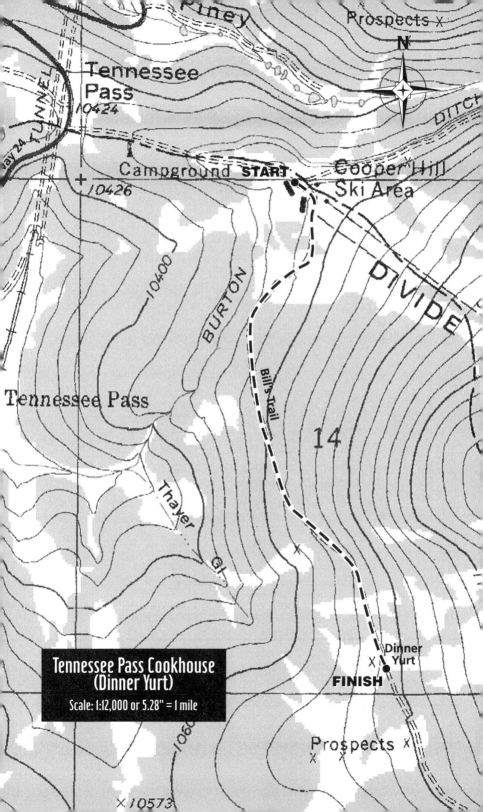

PINEY

Prospects ×

N

Hwy 24 TUNNEL

Tennessee Pass
10424

+ 10426

Campground **START** **Cooper Hill Ski Area**

DITCH

10400

BURTON

DIVIDE

Tennessee Pass

Bill's Trail

14

Thayer Gl.

Dinner Yurt
×

FINISH

Prospects ×
×

10573

1060

Tennessee Pass Cookhouse
(Dinner Yurt)
Scale: 1:12,000 or 5.28" = 1 mile

be temporary, the people at the Nordic Center decided a yurt built on eaves would do the trick. It's literally a gourmet restaurant that is temporarily permanent. Beginning at around Thanksgiving of each year, the Cookhouse opens for evening dinner guests and stays open until about the middle of April.

After a hard day of skiing/snowshoeing at the numerous backcountry areas in and around the Tennessee Pass area, or a day downhilling at the Cooper Ski Hill, or just visiting the scenic sights around Leadville—how about sitting down to a sumptuous dinner following a quick 15- to 30-minute cross-country ski or shoe trip? It's a trip that is both unusual and highly satisfying.

Bill's Trail to the Tennessee Pass Cookhouse is a standard 10 feet wide and meanders south and east across gentle rolling hills strewn with heavy woods along the Cooper Loop Trail. It's ideal for beginners because it gains only about 300 feet in elevation in just over 1.25 miles.

After leaving the Piney Creek Nordic Center at the Cooper Hill Ski Area, you head south along a well-marked trail. Continue south and then go east for about 0.75 mile. After you break out from the trees at

Directions at a glance

- The trailhead begins at the Piney Creek Nordic Center.

- Head south and then east along Bill's Trail approximately 1.0 mile to the Tennessee Pass Cookhouse.

- Enjoy a gourmet dinner and return to the trailhead back along the same route.

the top of the hill, you'll see the Cookhouse in an open meadow. Park your skis and walk to the yurt's deck where spectacular views of Mounts Elbert and Massive, the highest and second highest peaks in Colorado, greet you. Not to be outdone by the big tops, the Homestake Peak, Galena Peak, and Mt. of the Holy Cross also fill your view.

The trail, part of the larger Cooper Loop Trail which is in turn part of the U.S. Forest Service system, is regularly groomed and is ideal for skating or classic touring. Snowmobiles are also available to take disabled skiers/shoers and other visitors along the trail.

Guides will lead the group to the Tennessee Cookhouse each afternoon at around 5:30 P.M. Organized guided tours return about 9:00 P.M. However if you want to finish dinner and return early or hit the trails for a little private skiing/shoeing, you're welcome to use your headlamp and enjoy the star-filled night sky.

How to get there

From Denver go west on I–70 approximately 105 miles to the Minturn exit (171). This exit is approximately 5.4 miles west of Vail. At the bottom of the off-ramp, make a left and head south on U.S. Highway 24. Go approximately 24.5 miles to the top of Tennessee Pass. The turnoff to Cooper Hill Ski Area is on your left and at the top of the pass. Park by the Piney Creek Nordic Center.

From Leadville go north on Highway 24 approximately 8.8 miles to the Cooper Hill Ski Area and turn right. Drive to the Piney Creek Nordic Center at Ski Cooper and park. Check in at the Nordic Center.

Courtesy of Greater Leadville Area Chamber of Commerce

Treeline Loop

Tennessee Pass/Cooper Hill Ski Area, Leadville, CO

Type of trail:	▬▬ ⬭
Also used by:	Snowmobilers
Distance:	2.3 miles
Terrain:	Easy climbs and descents while meandering through lots of tree groves.
Trail difficulty:	Novice/beginner
Surface quality:	Ungroomed but often tracked by skiers/shoers.
Elevation:	10,424 at trailhead to over 10,600 at 1.0 mile
Time:	2 to 3 hours
Avalanche danger:	Low
Snowmobile use:	Low
Food and facilities:	It's less than 30 miles from Vail to the trailhead, and with some advance planning and reservations, there are always plenty of accommodations—however pricey—available. You can get brochure information on all of the overnight facilities by calling the Vail/Beaver Creek Reservations at (800) 525–2257. Vail also has a host of grocery stores, convenience stores, gas stations, and top restaurants to select from.

A more moderately priced option is to stay in Leadville, located less than 9 miles from the Treeline Loop trailhead. Hotel, motel, and bed-and-breakfast brochure information is available by calling the Leadville Chamber of Commerce at (719) 486–3900.

Complete equipment rentals and repairs can be found literally across the road at the Piney Creek Nordic Center located at the Cooper Hill Ski Area. For information on tours, guides, and equipment, call (719) 486–1750.

If you're coming in from the north, make sure you secure your gas, groceries, water, and snacks before leaving the Vail area. Likewise if you're coming from Leadville. Once you head off on the Treeline Loop Trail, there are no facilities.

The backcountry ski and snowshoe trails in the West Tennessee Pass are notoriously underutilized. Unlike the Front Range trails, which are close by to the more heavily populated areas, these trails around Leadville see relatively few people and lend skiers/snowshoers the full experience of an uncrowded great outdoors. Breaking trail is often the

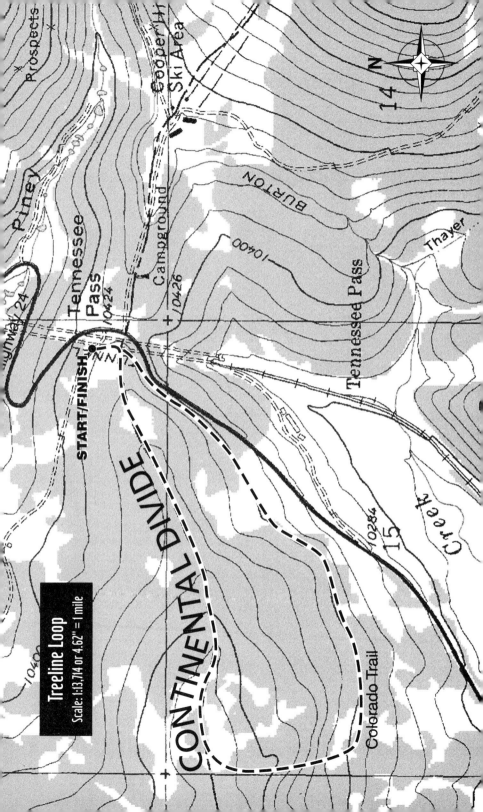

necessity and the joy of being the only group on the trail. Along with the solitude comes the responsibility to command good winter skills, along with map- and compass-reading knowledge.

As its name implies, the Treeline Loop Trail meanders mainly within glades of trees. Shaded from the wind, it is a fun, not-too demanding trail with gentle ascents and descents that let you experience the remoteness of the backcountry without having to be too far in the backcountry. Elevation grades all along the Treeline Loop Trail are all under 10 percent, good for the beginning skier/shoer.

There are no spectacular views of mountains here. The allure of the Treeline Loop Trail rests in being able to experience uncrowded forests and the quietness of nature. If you are observant in early morning or late afternoon, you might see a snowshoe hare, a porcupine, or squirrels and hear the call of birds that live in the area. Certainly telltale tracks in the snow will attest to deer, elk, and other wildlife also living nearby.

From the Tennessee Pass trailhead, the Treeline Loop follows the old Railroad Bed Road south for a short distance and then intersects with the Continental Divide. Follow the signs along the Railroad Bed Road for a short distance, watching for the signs that will head west along the Divide. Quite literally for the 1.0 mile you're traveling west, you can plant one ski or shoe on the eastern side of the

Directions at a glance

- Follow the old Railroad Bed Road from the trailhead. Signs will indicate it's the start of the Treeline Loop.

- Go 0.25 mile south on the old Railroad Bed Road and then turn west onto the Treeline Loop Trail.

- Trail literally follows along the top of the Continental Divide for approximately 1.0 mile.

- At the 1.0-mile mark, look for signs and trail that turns left and heads south.

- Go 0.25 mile south and head downhill until you intersect the Colorado Trail.

- Make a left and head east 1.0 mile on the Colorado Trail as it loops back to the trailhead.

Rocky Mountains and the other on the western side. Talk about being able to enjoy a case of Rocky Mountain high split personality!

After heading west for about 1.0 mile, look for a sign that will direct you to take the trail to the left and head south. Crossing just about anywhere in this general area will lead you gently down hill, and you'll intersect the Colorado Trail. From the Treeline Loop Trail heading south, you'll intersect the Colorado Trail in less than 0.25 mile. You'll traverse over a couple of small hills and open meadows.

When you intersect the Colorado Trail, make another left and head east. Again, it's a gentle traverse across the hillside for about 1.0 mile, and you will loop back around to the Tennessee Pass area. Once you're back at the trailhead, it's a simple job to cross the road and ski/shoe another 0.3 mile over to the Cooper Ski Hill Area for a warming cup of coffee or hot chocolate.

How to get there

From Denver go west on I–70 for approximately 105 miles to the Minturn exit (171). This exit is approximately 5.4 miles west of Vail. At the bottom of the off-ramp, make a left and head south on U.S. Highway 24. Go approximately 24.5 miles to the top of Tennessee Pass. Park on the west side of U.S. Highway 24. If there's no parking available, make a left into the Cooper Ski Hill area and park there.

From Leadville take Highway 24 north for approximately 8.8 miles to Tennessee Pass. Parking is available on either side of Highway 24 near Ski Cooper Hill area. The trailhead is located on the west side of Highway 24 along the Continental Divide. Or if you want to add an additional 0.3 mile to your route, you can park at the Ski Cooper Hill area and start the trail from the Piney Creek Nordic Center by heading west.

Tenth Mountain Division Hut

Leadville, CO

Type of trail:	▬▬▶ 🔘
Also used by:	Snowboarders
Distance:	9.0 miles
Terrain:	Challenging climbs and descents to the Hut, with great open bowls for skiing/trekking.
Trail difficulty:	Intermediate
Surface quality:	Ungroomed but sometimes tracked by skiers/shoers for first 1.5 miles. Then ungroomed backcountry conditions on rest of the route to the Hut.
Elevation:	Crane Lake Trailhead is at 10,196 feet and the hut is at 11,370 feet.
Time:	5 to 7 hours
Snowmobile use:	Low in area

Food and facilities: It's recommended that the route to the Tenth Mountain Division Hut be a destination point rather than a day trip. To make it to the hut, you may want to stay over in either Vail or Leadville the night before beginning your trek to the Tenth Mountain Division Hut. For information about the Tenth Mountain Division Hut and the system of huts, call (970) 925–5775. Advance reservations to stay over or use any of the facilities are required. Open for reservations from Thanksgiving until the end of April, the cost is $22 per person (plus tax), per night.

It's less than 30 miles from Vail to the trailhead, and with some advance planning and reservations, there are just about always plenty of accommodations available. You can get brochure information on all of the overnight facilities by calling the Vail/Beaver Creek Reservations at (800) 525–2257. Vail also has a host of grocery stores, convenience stores, gas stations, and top restaurants to select from.

A more moderately priced option is to stay in Leadville. Located less than 8 miles from the Crane Park trailhead, the accommodations and restaurant choices are not as "glitzy" as those found in Vail, but are certainly a lot more affordable. Hotel, motel, and bed-and-breakfast brochure information is available by calling the Leadville Chamber of Commerce at (719) 486–3900.

If you're coming from the north, make sure you secure your gas, groceries, water, and snacks before leaving the Vail area. If you're coming from Leadville, you'll also find the same facilities. Once you head off on the trail from Crane Park, there are no facilities.

This area is the home of the illustrious Tenth Mountain Division Hut System. The area surrounding the town of Leadville is historically important in the genesis of the sport of backcountry skiing in America. In 1942 the U.S. Army established Camp Hale just north of Leadville to house the Tenth Mountain Division, an elite ski-corps of commandos who trained for mountain combat against the Nazis in the European Alps. Also stationed there was the 99th Infantry Division. Made up of Norwegians and Norwegian expatriates, it was the only American division that included foreign citizens and was formed to aid the planned invasion of Norway.

For three winters, from 1942 to 1945, over 15,000 troops were stationed at Camp Hale. Unlike today's lightweight skis and gear, these Commandos had to wear 7-foot skis and 90-pound packs. Camouflaged

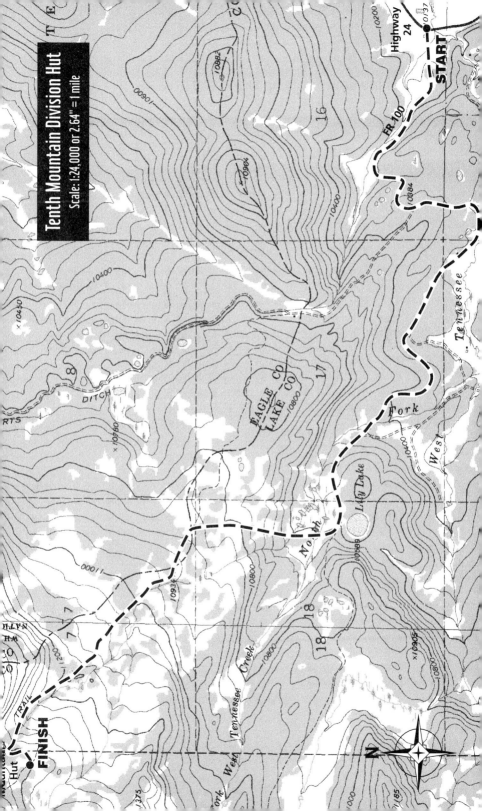

Tenth Mountain Division Hut

Scale: 1:24,000 or 2.64" = 1 mile

in winter-white suits, these "phantoms of the snow" practiced military exercises around what is now Ski Cooper and along the Gore and Sawatch ranges under conditions of military secrecy that would rival today's Top Secret Training bases!

After the war, and after being involved in many combat and commando missions, many of these soldiers came back to the Rocky Mountains where they had trained. Continuing to ski, they became instrumental in popularizing cross-country skiing as a sport and were often the major forces behind the development of early Colorado ski resorts. In 1982 the first Tenth Mountain Division Hut was erected. Today there are fourteen huts, and the system is renown as the most extensive and well laid-out of any in Colorado.

The overall favorite among strong backcountry skiers and snowshoers in the Leadville area is the trail to the Tenth Mountain Division Hut—a hut and trail that offers magnificent vistas of the 13,209-foot Homestake Peak to the west. Surrounding the hut are also great areas with deep powder ideal for practicing carving turns, snowshoe treks, and even some open bowl snowboarding. As with all the huts, the usual course of action is to spend the night there. The Tenth Mountain Division Hut offers accommodations for up to sixteen overnight skiers/shoers along with the standard cook stove, propane, lanterns, ice scoop, firewood, etc.

From the west side of U.S. Highway 24 at the Crane Lake turnout, look for the Forest Service sign to the Slide Lake Trail. It will be marked

Directions at a glance

- Trailhead begins at the Crane Lake turnout area and is marked FR 100.

- Ski/trek west on FR 100 for approximately 1.0 mile and look for Wurt's Ditch Road to intersect FR 100 from the north.

- Continue on FR 100 south and west for another 0.5 mile to the road that heads northwest to Lily Lake.

- Gentle ascent will take you over the North Fork of the West Tennessee Creek and around the north side of Lily Lake.

- On north side of Lily Lake, look for meadow on your right side (north).

- Ski across the meadow and pick up trail to Slide Creek and Slide Lake.

- Watch for blue diamond metal markers on the trees.

- Follow the blue diamonds to the Tenth Mountain Division Hut.

- Return on the same trail used to come into the area.

Photo by Ben Blankenburg, courtesy of Copper Mountain Resort

as Forest Road (FR) 100. Ski or snowshoe west on FR 100 about 1.0 mile. The FR 100 road will be intersected from the north by Wurt's Ditch Trail. Continue south on FR 100 and again west for another 0.5 mile.

At approximately the 1.5-mile mark from the trailhead, you'll choose the road that heads northwest toward Lily Lake (10,589-foot elevation). This part of the route continues a very gentle ascent on a grade of less than 8 percent and will take you over the North Fork of the West Tennessee Creek and around the north side of Lily Lake. Once you're on the north side of Lily Lake, look for a large, open, and flat meadow on your right (north). Continue skiing north, traversing this meadow until you pick up the trail which continues on the north side. The trail then veers sharply northeast and then back to the northwest, ascending through wooded hills. Watch carefully for the blue diamond metal signs that are used as trail markers on the trees. These blue diamonds will lead you directly north, across Slide Creek, and finally to the Tenth Mountain Division Hut.

Detailed topo maps, a compass, and a GPS unit to help navigate your way to the hut are essential. While the terrain is novice to intermediate at best, the greatest challenge is navigating through an area where there are a lot of trails that head in all directions.

The best route back to the trailhead is along the same route you used to come into the area.

How to get there

From Denver go west on I-70 approximately 105 miles to the Minturn exit, (171). This exit is approximately 5.4 miles west of Vail. At the bottom of the off-ramp, make a left and head south on U.S. Highway 24. Go over the top of Tennessee Pass and proceed another 1.6 miles to the Crane Park turnoff. Watch for signs indicating Forest Road 100.

From the town of Leadville, drive north on Highway 24 8.8 miles from the junction of CO 91 to the Crane Park turnoff. Parking is limited, and all vehicles need to park on the west side of Highway 24.

Aspen to Crested Butte via Pearl Pass

Ashcroft Ski Touring Center, Ashcroft/Aspen, CO

Type of trail:	▬▬▬▶
Distance:	25 miles one way; pick up shuttle vehicle at the end of the trail for the five-hour drive back to Aspen.
Terrain:	Extremely challenging climbs and descents from one end of the trail to the other.
Trail difficulty:	Expert
Surface quality:	Ungroomed backcountry conditions along entire route.
Elevation:	Trail starts at 9,498 feet, climbs to the top of Pearl Pass at 12,705 feet, and ends at East River Trailhead at 8,980 feet.
Time:	3 to 4 full days
Avalanche danger:	Moderate to extremely high.
Food and facilities:	A lot of advance planning is required for this trip. This is a journey that will tax even the most expert skier and back country adventurer. It is highly recommended that you consider hiring a guide through the professional services that can be found at Ute Mountaineer in Aspen. They can arrange for experienced guides, meals, and all the technical equipment needed to make the 25-mile trek a most memorable experience . . . and for all the right reasons! Contact the Ute Mountaineer at (970) 925–2849. Additional guiding service information can be obtained by calling Aspen Alpine Guides at (970) 925–6618. In Crested Butte call Adventures to the Edge at (970) 349–5219.

Reservations for the Tagert, Green-Wilson, and Friends Hut must be made in advance. If you have a guide or custom tour, they can take care of those arrangements for you. If you're doing it on your own, you can make reservations and get additional information and brochures by calling the Tenth Mountain Division Hut Association at (970) 925–5775.

Groceries, gas, snacks, and drinks are best obtained before leaving the Aspen area. In Aspen you'll find plenty of overnight accommodations with a choice of hotels, motels, bed-and-breakfasts, etc. For further information, call Aspen Central Reservations at (800) 262–7736.

To obtain your pass to go into the area, contact the Ashcroft Ski Touring Center at (970) 925–1971. For information about lunch or dinner reservations at the Pine Creek Cookhouse, call (970) 925–1044.

f you ask three different people about the same trail, you'll generally get three different opinions on how difficult it is, or how lengthy, or what the snow conditions are like. But this trail from Aspen to Crested Butte via Pearl Pass is a true classic route that every serious cross-country skier aspires to undertake. It's long. It's technically difficult. It takes you into the far reaches of the Elk Mountains and the Maroon Bells–Snowmass Wilderness Area. *This is an area where amateurs in map reading, route finding, avalanche safety, first aid, and basic winter survival skills should never venture.* But for those who are experienced in backcountry skiing and are up to the task, the route rewards them with untold beauty and challenge. This route is a character builder.

In fine weather you can ski it as a two-day trip, but the more practical thing to do, especially after a new snow when you have to break trail yourself, is plan on staying overnight at both the Tagert and Friends Huts along the way. The Tagert Hut, named for stage driver Billy Tagert, who drove pioneers, hopeful miners, and freight over Taylor Pass during the late 1800s, is located a little over 5.0 miles from the start of the tour. It makes for a short first day, with four to seven hours of skiing, and then a long second day of even more challenging technical skiing.

On the other side of Pearl Pass, you can stay at Friend's Hut. Because of the nature of this route, the strenuous climbs and descents, and the remoteness of the hut, it's best to go with a group of skiers and to reserve the hut for at least two days. *Starting at first light is a must and at least one member of the group must have skied the pass before and possess the skills to find the hut in whiteout conditions.* If you're a first-timer, it is strongly recommended you hire a professional guide.

This tour starts from the Ashcroft Touring Center as so many cross-country outings in this area do. From the trailhead ski south on the Castle Creek Road (FR 102) to the Pine Creek Cookhouse, and then to avoid dangerous avalanche chutes take the Ava-Pass route, which heads east across Castle Creek. Ski on that for about 0.5 mile, crossing back over the creek to intersect with the main road at the 2.0-mile point. You'll see a fork in the road. Be sure to take the right—or west—fork, heading south on the Castle Creek Road.

Be aware that Castle Creek is laden with avalanche gullies. The trail climbs southwest over two steep inclines, one, which rises about 700 feet in 1.0 mile, and several switchbacks. You'll pass the privately owned Mace Hut and then the cutoff to the Montezuma Mine before you veer to the south and ascend steep terrain to the Tagert or Green-Wilson Huts at a little over 5.3 miles from the trailhead.

The Tagert Hut and the Green-Wilson Hut are part of the Alfred Braun Hut System that's managed by the Tenth Mountain Division Hut Association. The Tagert Hut sleeps seven people, and the Green-Wilson Hut sleeps eight people. Both huts require a four-person minimum. Both huts in this system are rented only to one group at a time—hence the minimum number of overnight guests—and costs $17.50 per person, per night. After a good night's sleep, start at first light from the Tagert or Green-Wilson Hut to Pearl Pass by way of the Pearl Pass Road. Due to changing weather conditions much of this part of the tour is trekked over the path of least resistance. Basically you head south, staying to the east side of Pearl Pass basin, climbing and descending severe grades above treeline along the Cooper Creek Valley to the pass. The slope on the north side of the pass is the trickiest and takes you directly under an avalanche chute. Mountaineering skills are a must. For the last few hundred feet you'll climb up one person at a time—standard avalanche precaution. That way if the chute lets loose, only one person will be caught in the slide and the rest can effect a rescue.

Once you cross the pass, you'll descend quickly, heading southeast down an open basin for about 1.5 miles to the treeline. Turn south, skiing through the glades, which are at the upper end of the East Brush Creek Valley and east of Carbonate Hill. At East Brush Creek climb over the northwest fork through the trees to Friends Hut. It's about a 4.5-mile trek from the Tagert and Green-Wilson Huts to the Friends Hut. But don't let the relatively short distance fool you. It's going to take you a good 6 to 8 hours of hard skiing if the weather conditions are anything but ideal.

Built in honor of ten people who were killed in a midair collision over East Maroon Pass, the Friends Hut has given shelter to many a skier venturing over the pass since 1985. As with most huts, it contains a wood stove, a propane cook stove, firewood, cookware, mattresses, and dishes. Light is supplied by a photovoltaic system, and water is obtained by melting snow. No dogs are allowed. The cost is $15 per person, per night, and eight people can sleep comfortably. More than one group can be booked at a time, so if you want the cabin to yourselves, you can reserve it for $100 per night.

The second half of the route from Friend's Hut to the East River trailhead near Crested Butte begins through the thick stands of trees, heading south. Descending along a creek bed for approximately 0.75 mile, you'll meet up with the Brush Creek Trail and veer to the southwest, eventually arriving at Brush Creek Valley just under 6.0 miles from Friends Hut. If snow conditions are right, stay with the four-wheel-drive vehicle trail and head southwest over the open valley bottom, then traversing west and southwest across the south rim of Teocalli Ridge.

Directions at a glance

- Park in the parking area near the Toklat Lodge. Get a trail pass from the Ashcroft Ski Touring Center.

- The trailhead to Pearl Pass Hut leads south along FR 102 from the parking area. Starting at first light is a must.

- Continue on trail approximately 1.5 miles and look for the Pine Creek Cookhouse. Good spot for coffee break, but reservations for lunch and dinner are suggested.

- After the Pine Creek Cookhouse, look for Ava-Pass route, which takes you off the road and down into the Castle Creek area, to avoid known avalanche chutes.

- Ski back on the road at approximately the 2.0-mile mark.

- Trail will divide. Take the trail to the right and continue to head south and west on the Castle Creek Road (FR 102). Be aware of avalanche gullies in Castle Creek. Watch for the privately owned Mace Hut, and the cutoff to the Montezuma Mine. From where the trail divides, it's about 3.0 miles until you see the Tagert and Green-Wilson Huts.

- After your overnight stay, at first light head south on Pearl Pass Road from the huts, staying along the Cooper Creek Valley to the top of Pearl Pass. It's about 2.75 miles, but it's steep, and it takes you directly under an avalanche chute.

- At Pearl Pass you'll head southeast for about 1.5 miles to treeline at the upper end of the East Brush Creek Valley and east of Carbonate Hill.

- At East Brush Creek, climb past the northwest fork and stop for the night at Friends Hut.

- Head south from Friends Hut for approximately 0.75 mile and intersect the Brush Creek Trail. Veer to the southwest and continue down along the trail for approximately 5.0 miles.

- Traverse west and southwest along Teocalli Ridge and continue southwest another 4.0 miles to the Brush Creek Cow Camp.

- Continue southwest into the East River Valley along the main 4x4-vehicle road. Another 3.0 miles pass the Cold Spring Ranch, and you'll come to the East River trailhead.

- Pick up your shuttle vehicles and it's about a five-hour winter drive back to Aspen.

Stay on the trail, heading southwest to intersect with another trail. Keep heading southwest until you pass the Brush Creek Cow Camp. Not much to see here, but the fences and pens will give you a good bearing, and you'll be able to note that you've now gone just over 10.0 miles for the day—luckily most of it has been downhill. Just past the Brush Creek Cow Camp is the junction of the Brush Creek and East River Valleys. It is a 4-wheel-drive vehicle road. Head south over a valley that mercifully is pretty level to the Cold Spring Ranch. Just a little farther ahead to the southwest is the East River trailhead. Here is where you leave your shuttle cars parked for the nearly five-hour drive back to Aspen.

How to get there

From Aspen go west on Highway 82 approximately 0.75 mile. Turn left onto Maroon Creek Road, then immediately turn left onto Castle Creek Road. It's also marked as Forest Road (FR) 102. Drive on the winding Castle Creek Road for approximately 12.0 miles and park near the Toklat Lodge at the lot marked for the trail on the left, or east, side of the road. The parking area is pretty large, so finding a spot is usually not a problem.

Photo by Tari and Andy Lightbody

Lindley Hut

Ashcroft Ski Touring Center, Ashcroft/Aspen, CO

Type of trail:	▬▬▬▬ ⬭⬭⬭
Distance:	8.0 miles
Terrain:	Easy to moderate climbs and descents from one end of the trail to the other.
Trail difficulty:	Novice/intermediate
Surface quality:	Ungroomed but sometimes tracked by skiers/shoers.
Elevation:	Trail starts at 9,498 feet and ends at 10,624 feet at the Lindley Hut.
Time:	3 to 5 hours
Snowmobile use:	Low
Avalanche danger:	Extreme potential for avalanches exists along the trail.
Food and facilities:	If you're planning on staying overnight at the Lindley Hut, advance reservations are required. Additional information and brochures can be obtained by calling the Tenth Mountain Division Hut Association at (970) 925-5775. The hut opens for overnight guests around Thanksgiving, but requires a minimum of six people in a group for reservations.

Groceries, gas, snacks, and drinks are best obtained before leaving the Aspen area. In Aspen you'll find plenty of overnight accommodations with a choice of hotels, motels, bed-and-breakfasts, etc. For further information, call Aspen Central Reservations at (800) 262-7736.

To obtain your pass to go into the area, contact the Ashcroft Ski Touring Center at (970) 925-1971. For information about lunch or dinner reservations at the Pine Creek Cookhouse, call (970) 925-1044. For guides and customized tours, call Aspen Alpine Guides at (970) 925-6618. For equipment rentals and repairs call the Aspen Cross-Country Center at (970) 925-2145 or Ute Mountaineers at (970) 925-2849.

L ocated in the spectacularly rugged Elk Mountains, the trails stemming from the Aspen area enter into remote and difficult terrain where skills of route finding and avalanche safety and intermediate skiing ability are a must. The trail to the Lindley Hut is technically one of the easier trails in this area. The first half of the route is relatively flat and well marked to avoid dangerous avalanche chutes. The second half of the

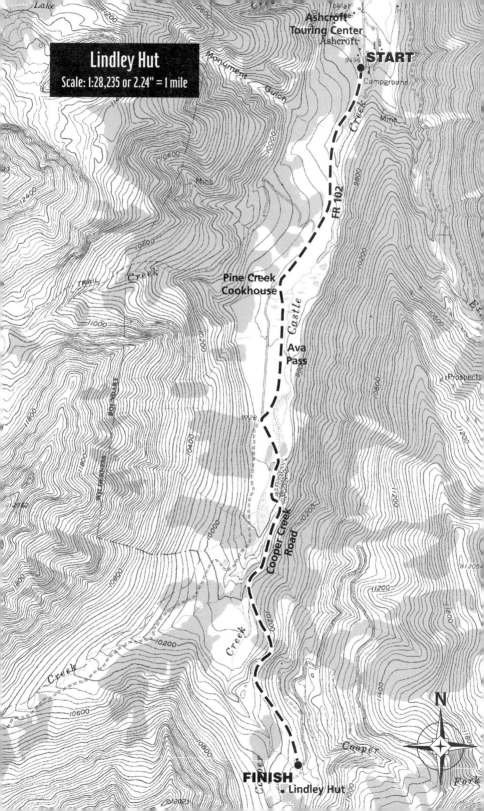

trail follows a road offering a climb that snowshoers will enjoy and skiers will have to work at. The trail leaves the road sometime during the second half and some route finding will be necessary.

The Lindley Hut is actually the largest in the Braun Memorial Hut System and can accommodate up to twelve people. Like most huts it offers a wood-burning stove for heat. Water is obtained by melting snow. Because the area is so isolated and skiers/shoers can easily trigger avalanches, for safety reasons a minimum of six people are required to reserve the hut overnight.

Before you start your tour you need to get a trail pass at the Ashcroft Ski Touring Center. From the trailhead at the center, ski or snowshoe south on the Castle Creek Road—also marked as FR 102—up over a couple of moderate hills to the Pine Creek Cookhouse at about 1.5 miles from the trailhead. The Pine Creek Cookhouse is a good spot for lunch and dinner, but it's often crowded, so advance reservations are suggested. You normally can stop off and at least get a cup of hot chocolate or coffee while enroute.

Directions at a glance

- Park in the parking area near the Toklat Lodge. Get a trail pass from the Ashcroft Ski Touring Center.
- The trailhead to Lindley Hut leads south along FR 102 from the parking area.
- Continue on the trail approximately 1.5 miles and look for the Pine Creek Cookhouse. Good spot for a coffee break. Reservations for lunch and dinner are suggested.
- After the Pine Creek Cookhouse, look for Ava-Pass route that takes you off the road and down into the Castle Creek area. This trail avoids known avalanche chutes.
- Ski back on road at approximately the 2.0-mile mark. Look for the fork in the trail. Take the trail to the east—or left—and follow the Cooper Creek Road.
- Steady climbing of from 12 percent to 20 percent grades for next 1.75 miles. Be aware the avalanche danger does exist.
- When the trail breaks into open area on top, and the trail/road U-turns to the north, leave the trail and begin heading south an eighth of a mile to the Lindley Hut.
- To return to the trailhead, take the same route back down.

After the Pine Creek Cookhouse, you'll see a lot of signs warning of the avalanche dangers and an Ava-Pass Trail intersection where you leave the road and head east across Castle Creek before bending back around to the south to intersect with the road again at the 2.0-mile point. The Ava-Pass Trail is well marked and takes you out of the paths of known chutes.

Once you get back on the road, look for the trail to fork. The trail to the right leads farther down Castle Creek and is the route for advanced skiers who are heading up over Pearl Pass. If you are on your way to Lindley Hut, you will want the east or left fork, which is Cooper Creek Road, and head south. Steadily climbing up hefty 12 percent to 20 percent grades, you'll go 1.75 miles, winding in and out of the trees. On the left will be slopes with a potential for avalanches so take extreme care. Avalanche beacons and snow shovels should be part of your standard equipment.

When the terrain levels at the top of the last rise and the road U-turns to the north, it's time to leave the road and head south the last eighth of a mile to Lindley Hut. After you leave the road, you'll cross over a bridge that spans Cooper Creek. There'll be a switchback that veers to the west, then south, and finally east to the cabin. The hut lies near the creek, and because of its size, it's easy to spot.

To return to the trailhead, take the same route back and enjoy the gentle downhill glide and trek.

How to get there

From Aspen go west on Highway 82 approximately 0.75 mile. Turn left onto Maroon Creek Road, and then immediately turn left onto Castle Creek Road. It's also marked as Forest Road (FR) 102. Drive on the winding Castle Creek Road for approximately 12.0 miles and park near the Toklat Lodge at the lot marked for the trail on the left, or east, side of the road. The parking area is pretty large, so finding a spot is usually not a problem.

Sunlight/Babbish Gulch

Sunlight Mountain Ski Resort, Glenwood Springs, CO

Type of trail:	▬▬▬ ⬤⬤⬤
Also used by:	Some downhill skiers and snowboarders
Distance:	Lower Trail loop—10.0 miles Lower and Upper Trail loops combined—18.0 miles.
Terrain:	Easy and gradual first several miles. Then moderate climbs and descents throughout Lower Trail loop.
Trail difficulty:	Intermediate
Surface quality:	Lower Trail loop groomed and maintained by Sunlight Ski Resort. Upper Trail ungroomed but often tracked by skiers/shoers.
Elevation:	Trailhead 7,800 feet, climbs to 9,600 feet
Time:	3 hours to full day
Avalanche danger:	Low
Food and facilities:	Trail is located close to Glenwood Springs, where there are many fine restaurants, lounges, grocery stores, and overnight accommodations. It's also located at the base of the Sunlight Mountain Ski Resort area so there are plenty of rooms, condos, and restaurants conveniently located at the starting/stopping point of the trail. For complete snowshoeing/ski information, call the Sunlight Ski Resort (800–445–7931). Additional overnight accommodations can be made at the resort area through the Sunlight Mountain Inn (800–733–4757) and the Brettelberg Inn (800–634–0481).

While the Sunlight Mountain Ski Resort has four lifts for downhill skiing and charges a daily fee, they also maintain just over 10.0 miles of backcountry cross-country ski/snowshoe trails that are available to everyone at no charge. The trailhead begins at the resort, and the lower loop is groomed and maintained throughout the season. The 10.0-mile loop is rated as intermediate. The trail runs to the east for the first 0.5 mile along the relatively flat Old Fourmile Road, which turns into Williams (Road) Trail. Here is where it becomes steeper and starts climbing uphill to the south. The loop follows a summertime horseback/llama path and is a combination of moderate up- and downhill climbs with a wide, well-marked trail, surrounded by groves of aspen and pine trees. You'll see plenty of tree squirrels and even an occasional blue grouse along the trail. The tree stands are thick and mature—providing a good

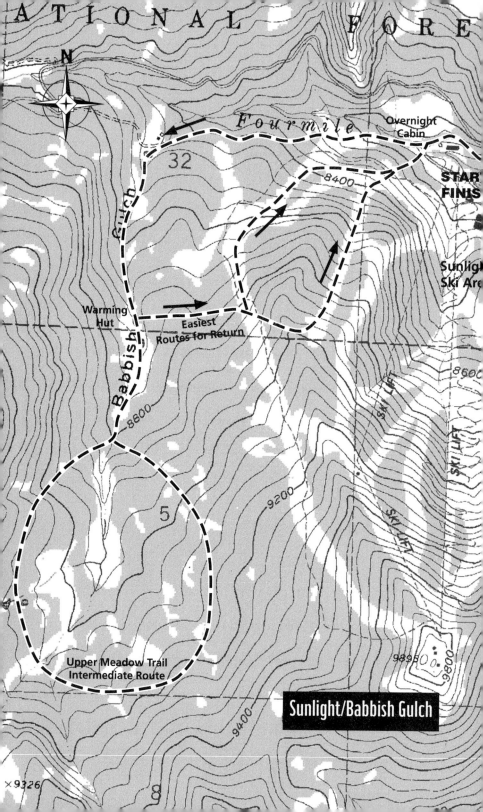

windbreak even when the weather is blustery. A lot of smaller ungroomed and unmarked trails inside this main loop cut diagonally off the main trail if you're looking for shortcuts that are not crowded!

Approximately 5 miles up the Williams Trail is a small warming hut/rest area. There are no facilities here, but it's a good opportunity to take a break at this halfway point. Get out of the weather and off the trail, sit inside on the hardwood floor, and enjoy a sack lunch. The trail divides at this warming hut and offers three options: You can follow the markers that connect with the Dipsy Doodle Trail to the northeast. This trail will continue the loop back down the mountain and bring you back to the Sunlight/Fourmile trailhead. The second option is to take the groomed trail that sidecuts the mountain to the east and intersects with the resort's downhill ski area, called the Ute Downhill run. Your last

Directions at a glance

- Trail routes begin at the edge of the Sunlight Mountain Resort parking lot to the east. At 0.25 mile there is a rustic cabin along the Fourmile Road. Continue past the cabin another 0.25 mile to Williams Trail.
- Trail heads south and climbs up through conifers and aspen trees.
- At top of trail, at approximately 5 miles, there is a warming hut for a rest stop and lunch. No facilities here.
- From the warming hut follow the marked trail northeast and intersect the marked Dipsy Doodle Trail. Head downhill on it back to the Sunlight/Babbish Gulch trailhead.

Alternate route 1

- Ski/shoe east from the warming hut and intersect the downhill ski run.
- Ski/shoe down the ski run to return to the trailhead at the Sunlight Ski Resort.

Alternate route 2

- From the warming hut continue south to the higher Upper Meadows Trail.
- These trails are ungroomed and provide backcountry trailblazing opportunities.
- Trails all loop back down to the warming hut. Take Dipsy Doodle trail from the warming hut back downhill to trailhead.

option is to continue from the warming hut, going higher on the Upper Meadows Trail, which allows you to head into the backcountry on non-groomed snow.

This additional 8.0-mile Upper Meadows loop is also rated as intermediate, but it provides a more challenging backcountry experience because you can break your own trail or travel less-used terrain. The Upper Meadows loop begins and ends at the warming hut/rest area and enables you at the day's end to enjoy mostly downhill terrain on groomed snow back to the trailhead after an afternoon of trailblazing.

Approximately a quarter mile to the east from the trailhead, located alongside the Old Fourmile Road, is a rustic cabin that can be rented on a nightly basis from the resort. Cost is $40 per night for your entire group. The cabin will sleep up to eight people, and at $40 per night for everyone, this is a real backcountry bargain. The resort provides firewood for heating and cooking as well as electricity. An outhouse is nearby, and you have to provide all of your own sleeping bags, cooking gear, etc. If you're looking for more civilized accommodations, the Sunlight Mountain Inn has bed-and-breakfast style lodging, while the Brettelberg Inn offers a host of condominiums.

How to get there

From Glenwood Springs take Grand Avenue south from I–70 to County Road 117 and proceed about 10 miles to the Sunlight Mountain Ski Resort area. Trailhead is marked as both Sunlight/Four Mile and is located atop Babbish Gulch on Compass Peak, approximately 10 miles south of Glenwood Springs. There is plenty of parking in the lot, where you'll see the Sunlight Mountain Ski Resort as well as the Sunlight Mountain Inn and the Brettelberg Inn.

Photo by Tom Stillo, courtesy of Crested Butte Mountain Resort

Powderhorn

Mesa Lakes Resort, Grand Junction, CO

Type of trail:	▬▬ ⬭
Distance:	7.0 to 12.0 miles
Terrain:	Gradual climbs all along the trail ridge, and great downhill runs to the Powderhorn Ski Resort.
Trail difficulty:	Intermediate
Surface quality:	Ungroomed but usually tracked by skiers/shoers along the trail and ridgeline. Packed and groomed downhill runs at the Ski Resort.
Elevation:	Trailhead 9,870 feet to Powderhorn Ski Resort Ridge at 9,700 feet
Time:	3 hours to full day
Avalanche danger:	Low
Food and facilities:	Mesa Lakes Resort is open year-round and serves winter users. Downhill, cross-country, and snowshoe equipment, clothing, and accessories are available through their rental ski shop. For overnight information or a brochure on their facilities, call the Mesa Lakes Resort at (970) 268–5467. Gas, groceries, other restaurants, and a liquor store are located 14 miles back up Highway 65 in Mesa. At the Powderhorn Ski Resort you'll also find overnight accommodations, restaurants, and lounges. For a brochure and more information about the Powderhorn Ski Resort, call them at (970) 268–5700.

The Grand Mesa region is a mecca for snowmobilers in the state. Literally hundreds of miles of trails run all across this giant flat-top mountain. Many miles of these trails are shared by cross-country skiers, and snowshoers out on day trips. Although trails are well marked and well groomed thanks to high-horsepower tracked machines, they are often very crowded, and solitude is rare.

About an hour from Grand Junction, you'll find an area that is scenic and activity rich but does not have snowmobile traffic competing for the trail. The West Bench Trail that begins at the Mesa Lakes Resort is rated for intermediate skiers and snowshoers, and has *no* snowmobile traffic! The trailhead begins at the Mesa Lakes Resort (970–268–5467). It's well marked and is designated on the topographic maps as TR 501. The West

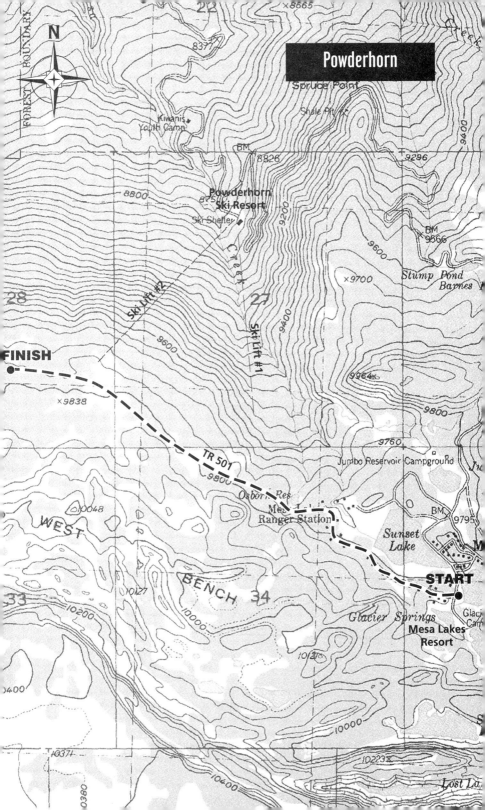

Bench Trail is a ridgeline route with a nearly constant series of small to moderate up- and downhill climbs and glides. The trail is marked with both Forest Service tree patches and occasional signage.

Stay along the top of the ridge, and the trail will take you through small breaks that are lined with groves of aspen and spruce trees. When the weather turns blustery, the trees provide an excellent windbreak, and blowing snow across the path is minimal. Approximately 3.5 miles from the trailhead, the path opens up and climbs gently to the top of the number 1 ski lift at the Powderhorn Ski Resort. Here snowshoers, cross-country skiers, or telemark users can check in with the lift operators and receive a "token" that enables them to ski or shoe down to the Powderhorn Ski Resort for lunch and a little rest and relaxation. Then they can ride the lift back up for free!

Directions at a glance

- The West Bench trailhead begins in the parking lot of the Mesa Lakes Resort and is marked TR 501.
- Stay along the top of the ridge, head west and watch for occasional Forest Service wood signs and tree patches.
- Continue to ridgeline west for approximately 3.5 miles and look for the top of the Powderhorn Ski Resort lift 1. Get "return token" from ski operators and ski to base for lunch.
- Return route is by riding the ski lift back up the mountain and following trail back to Mesa Lakes Resort.

Alternate route

- If you don't want to go down ski lift 1, continue on the West Bench Trail heading west for another 2.5 miles to ski lift 2.
- Get a return token from ski lift operator and ski down to base of Powderhorn Ski Resort for lunch, or turn around and ski/trek approximately 6.0 miles back to the trailhead at the Mesa Lakes Resort.

If you're not ready to head down to the ski resort, continue on the West Bench Trail, which continues to follow the ridge line. The trail is still at the intermediate level and is for the most part pretty flat. It's an area that's good for level to mild rolling ridges, gentle shoeing, and glide skiing. Ahead 2.5 miles is the top of the number 2 ski lift at the Powderhorn Ski Resort. Once again check in with the lift operators and secure your free lift token before heading down the hill.

If you want to start at the Powderhorn Ski Resort, a one-trip "up the lift" pass will cost $10. While many of the lifts in Colorado will let cross-country skiers and snowshoers use their resort runs to come down from higher elevations, many have restrictions about allowing this kind of winter sports recreation to start on the commercial downhill ski lifts. The Powderhorn Ski Resort is one that welcomes all outdoor winter recreationalists. At the top of either the number 1 or number 2 ski lift, you can reverse the ridge course along the West Bench Trail and work back to the trail head at the Mesa Lakes Resort.

At the Mesa Lakes Resort, parking and access to all of the cross-country/snowshoe trails are free. Overnight accommodations at the resort begin at $45 for a motel room and go up to $150 for cabins that will sleep up to twelve people.

How to get there

From Grand Junction take I–70 East approximately 12 miles to highway 65. Head toward the Powderhorn Ski Resort. Stay on Highway 65 for approximately 25 miles and park at the Mesa Lakes Resort. This is approximately 4.5 miles after passing the Powderhorn Ski Resort. The trailhead for the West Bench Trail begins at the edge of the Mesa Lakes Resort and is well marked.

Old Monarch Pass

Salida, CO

Type of trail:	▬▬▬ 🏂
Also used by:	Snowmobilers
Distance:	3.0 miles to 21.0 miles, depending on trail chosen
Terrain:	Gradual climb at the beginning, and great downhill runs/trails down to where you leave the shuttle car.
Trail difficulty:	Moderate to advanced, depending on trail chosen
Surface quality:	Ungroomed but usually well tracked by skiers/shoers.
Elevation:	Trailhead 11,500 to 10,300 feet; elevation change 300 to 2,400 feet, depending on trail chosen
Time:	2 hours to all day
Avalanche danger:	Low to moderate
Snowmobile use:	Moderate to heavy, depending on tour chosen
Food and facilities:	Use restaurant and gas facilities before leaving Salida. At the Monarch Ski Resort there are a restaurant, bar, and cafeteria open to the public. The Monarch Mountain Lodge, about 4.5 miles back down the hill from the ski slope area, has nice modern rooms, very reasonable rates, and a great restaurant and bar in which to unwind. For package information call (800) 332–3668.

Old Monarch Pass offers great snow conditions and an opportunity to practice every sort of skiing or snowshoeing. If you only want to ski for half a day, just head out from the trailhead for 1.5 miles to the old pass location. You'll see an open park that's great for mastering flat-track techniques. The trail is rated easy to moderate and lined with giant pines and conifer trees. If you want to try out powder or cut some telemark turns, head up the small peak to the south of the old pass and carve your way down to the park.

For those who might want the challenge of an all-day tour, just continue down the west side of the pass for 9.0 miles of gliding or downhill shoeing on a 5 percent grade above No Name Creek. Here is where you'll find that shuttle vehicle you parked down below to come in very handy and save you a long haul back up the hill.

Because you're skiing or shoeing on the east side of Monarch Pass, you'll be skiing right next to the Monarch Ski Area. It's marked with a boundary rope, and fast-flying downhill skiers will often cruise right past

you. This happens only for a small section of the trail, and as long as both groups stay on their sides of the rope, there shouldn't be any trouble.

The fun thing about this trail is that it has a history dating back to 1879 and was used by mountain travelers and miners in search of gold. In truth the trail was in use for hundreds of years or more and long before that by the Ute Indians, who once lived, hiked, and traveled these mountains.

How to get there

From Salida drive approximately 14 miles west on Highway 50 toward Gunnison. Go past the Monarch Ski Resort for approximately 0.7 mile and look for a highway sign on your right that reads OLD MONARCH PASS. Parking area at the trailhead is usually plowed and provides parking for up to 12–15 vehicles.

To get your shuttle vehicle to the end of the route, go 8.8 miles west from the trailhead parking area up over the Monarch Pass Summit on Highway 50. Drop down to the western side of the pass and look for the White Pine Road on the Gunnison–Saguache county line. Make a right and go north on White Pine Road for 4.7 miles. Then get on Old Monarch Pass heading east until you hit the snow closure. Parking here is sparse. When you leave your vehicle, park it so others can get around. Reverse the trip back up to Monarch Pass and start your skiing or snowshoeing at the trailhead pullout/parking area.

Directions at a glance

- From the trailhead parking area, begin a gradual ascent up the Old Monarch Pass road.

- Approximately 1.5 miles from the trailhead, the route opens up into a meadow park. Numerous small cuts are available to trek or ski through.

- Continue on the road to the west side of the pass. Nine miles of gentle switchbacks at no more than 5 percent grade will guide you down to where you left your shuttle vehicle. Take care not to drift into the Monarch Ski Area.

Washington Gulch to Elkton Cabin

Crested Butte, CO

Type of trail:	▬▬ 🏂
Also used by:	Snowmobilers
Distance:	10.4 miles
Terrain:	Level to rolling with gradual climbs to the Cabin.
Trail difficulty:	Novice to intermediate
Surface quality:	Ungroomed but usually well tracked by skiers/shoers.
Elevation:	Trailhead 9,450 to 10,700 feet; elevation gain moderate, averaging about 200 feet per mile
Time:	3 to 5 hours
Avalanche danger:	Low
Snowmobile use:	Medium
Food and facilities:	The Crested Butte Marketplace is located on County Road 317, about 0.5 mile before the turn-off to Washington Gulch/Meridian Lake. It has a gas station and small mini-market/grille. Dry goods groceries are available, as are sack lunches and plenty of bottled drinks. If you're looking for a place for a sit-down lunch or dinner, the town of Mount Crested Butte offers a host of fine eateries, as does the historical town of Crested Butte. For more information on Crested Butte trails, contact the Crested Butte Nordic Center (970–349–1707); to reserve the Elkton Cabin, call Adventures to the Edge Limited (970–349–5219).

Surrounded by the majestic vistas of the Elk Mountains, the West Elks, and the Ruby–Anthracite Range, Crested Butte is a haven for Nordic skiers and is thought by many to be the birthplace of the modern American telemark turn. Over the same routes used by mountain bikers during the summer, winter outdoor enthusiasts can choose among a myriad of trails and three huts, Elkton, Gothic, and Friends, to either base camp at or stay the night.

The trail to the abandoned mining camp of Elkton is a well-established, popular route shared by snowmobilers, snowshoers, telemarkers, and cross-country skiers. The best time to go is after a fresh snow when you can break trail yourself and enjoy the calm and peace of the gently rolling terrain.

From the parking area and trailhead signs (FR 811), you ski or snowshoe up the valley over level to rolling terrain that's ideal for the begin-

Washington Gulch to Elkton Cabin
Scale: 1:43,636 or 1.45" = 1 mile

FINISH

Elkton Cabin

FR 881

STAR

Directions at a glance

- Trail begins at the parking lot and is marked as FR 811. Follow FR 811 up through Washington Gulch. At about 2.0 miles you'll see the Meridian Lake on your left.

- For the next 3.0 miles the trail continues along FR 811 up through Washington Gulch with a steady climb.

- The climb gets steeper for last 0.5 mile before reaching the abandoned town of Elkton. Look for the cabin closest to the trail, which can be rented for day use or overnight stays.

- Return to the trailhead following the same 5.2-mile route back downhill to your car.

ner and intermediate skier or shoer. After touring the easy-to-follow Washington Gulch Road, you'll come to a sustained climb at the 3.0-mile marker near the southwest corner of Gothic Mountain. Once past this section, the road climbs gradually, passing below the mountain's southwest face. From here, the terrain becomes increasingly steep as you cross the mouth of a drainage to the northeast, then turn west (left) and south (left) across a creek and the head of Washington Gulch.

After crossing the creek, make the final climb to Elkton by ascending a switchback, heading northwest. When you arrive, you'll see two cabins off to the right. The first cabin, the one closest to the road, is Elkton Cabin. With a wood-burning stove for heat, a gas stove for cooking, an outhouse, and directions to a nearby water supply, this cabin makes a convenient base camp for a day trip, but reservations are required.

Spend the day hiking, skiing, and exploring the area that was once famous for its late 1880s and early 1990s mining operations. If you're not staying overnight at the Elkton Cabin, it's a nice gentle glide or trek back down the same route to the trailhead.

How to get there

The well-marked trailhead is at end of a county road near the Meridian Lakes Development. From the stop sign at the intersection of Elk Avenue and County Road 317 in Crested Butte (Highway 135 turns into County Road 317), drive north for 1.7 miles to the Washington Gulch and Meridian Lakes turnoff. Turn left onto Washington Gulch Road (FR 811) and proceed along the main road to the plowed parking area at the winter road closure.

Rainbow Lake

Gunnison, CO

Type of trail:	▬▬ 🏔, ◀ nearby
Also used by:	Snowmobilers
Distance:	22.0 miles
Terrain:	Level road with lots of rolling gentle hills.
Trail difficulty:	Easy/novice
Surface quality:	Ungroomed but sometimes tracked by skiers/shoers.
Elevation:	Trailhead at 7,600 feet, climbs to 10,900 feet at Rainbow Lake
Time:	4 hours to full day
Avalanche danger:	Low
Snowmobile use:	Low
Food and facilities:	The Rainbow Lake Road trail is located about 13 miles west of Gunnison, which has many fine restaurants, overnight accommodations, grocery stores, etc. Fill up your car with gas and get all of your snacks, lunches, and drinks before leaving town. Best place for meals and accommodations on the west end of town is at the Silver Spur Restaurant and the EconoLodge. You can call the Silver Spur Restaurant for information (970–641–5301), or the recently renovated and remodeled EconoLodge (970–641–1000).

Call the Gunnison County Chamber of Commerce (970–641–1501) for brochures and information about other winter skiing/snowshoeing and outdoor activities. If you're planning on ice fishing in the area, manual and gas-powered ice augers and rental gear are available through Gunnison Sporting Goods (970–641–5022).

The Rainbow Lake Road has what is called a "very extreme" southern exposure. Because of this, light snows often melt quickly. If the area has a heavy snow and snow pack, it is an excellent and scenic trail from around Christmas until early April. If the snow is sparse, the trail can be spotty and even muddy, especially in the late spring. Mid- to late winter months are by far the best for using this uncrowded trail.

Beginning at the snow closure gate, the Rainbow Lake Road climbs very gently and steadily up through wide-open sagebrush country into a small canyon that follows the East Fork of Dry Creek. Small groves of aspen trees mark your ascent. As the canyon narrows, prehistoric rock

pillars dot the landscape above you, and there are leftover, eroded mud columns that date back nearly one hundred million years. In eons past the area was covered with boiling hot mud from a nearby volcano. Much of it has eroded away, but spires are still left as remnants. The very unusual geologic formations provide great photo opportunities.

Elevation increases are gradual on the Rainbow Lake Road, but there are a lot of up- and downhill ridges. These ridges continue all the way up to Rainbow Lake where the terrain changes from sagebrush and aspen tree groves to conifer stands.

All along the Rainbow Lake Road, you will often get to view Dry Creek. In truth it is anything but dry and is dotted with countless small beaver ponds, dams, and huts.

Lower elevations—the first 2 to 5 miles—are favorite wintering grounds for hundreds of resident deer and elk. Wildlife viewing opportunities are fantastic. A good set of binoculars and a camera with lots of film should be considered a "must," part of everyone's standard equipment.

One of the nice features about this trail is that you can turn around and go back just about anywhere along the route that's convenient or comfortable. Simply turn around and enjoy the gentle hills and gradual descent back to the trailhead.

Once you get back to your parked vehicle, you may be interested in the frozen Blue Mesa Reservoir across Highway 50. You may enjoy walking downhill less than a quarter mile to the lake and practicing skate skiing, flatland snowshoeing, and even a little ice fishing! When the Blue Mesa Reservoir is frozen, it provides nearly 100 miles of totally uncrowded shoreline skate-skiing, shoeing, and angling. Many winter enthusiasts ski or shoe

Directions at a glance

- Trailhead begins at the road closure sign and is marked Forest Route (FR) 724.

- Trail makes a gentle uphill ascent and goes along the East Fork of Dry Creek.

- Trail continues on FR 724 for just over 11 miles with lots of small up- and downhill ridges.

- To return trek or ski back very gentle downhill slopes and ridges to trailhead.

out on the lake early in the morning, drill a few holes, and do a little through-the-ice fishing for rainbows, brown trout, lake trout, and Kokanee salmon. Then after an early morning of angling, skate-skiing, or shoeing, it's time to begin a scenic midmorning journey back up along Rainbow Lake Road.

How to get there

From the city of Gunnison head west on Highway 50 approximately 13 miles to the Rainbow Lake Road turnoff. Road is well marked with Park Service signs. Turnout for Rainbow Lake Road will be on your right. Park Service/Forest Service road closure signs are located less than a quarter mile from Highway 50. Although the area is open to snowmobiles, because of snow closure signs, snowmobile use is very low.

Photo by Ken Missbrenner, courtesy of Aspen Skiing Company

Kebler Pass to Lake Irwin

Mount Crested Butte, CO

Type of trail:	▬▬▬ ⚙
Also used by:	Snowmobilers
Distance:	14.0 miles
Terrain:	Level road with gentle grade and then moderately challenging ascents to the lodge.
Trail difficulty:	Easy/novice for first 5 miles; intermediate for last 2 miles to lodge (difficult trails also available)
Surface quality:	Ungroomed but almost always well tracked by skiers/shoers.
Elevation:	Trailhead 9,208 feet, climbs to 10,420 feet at the Lake Irwin Lodge
Time:	3 to 5 hours
Avalanche danger:	Low
Snowmobile use:	Medium to high
Food and facilities:	Irwin Lodge is open year-round for lodging, meals, lounge, sack lunches, and all the amenities of a great resort. For lodging information and a brochure, call the Irwin Lodge at (970–349–9800). Two miles east is the town of Crested Butte, recognized as a National Historic District. It has great hotels, plenty of charming bed-and-breakfast establishments, grocery stores, plenty of ski rental shops, and fine gourmet restaurants. For further information about accommodations and additional cross-country ski/snowshoe trails and tours in Crested Butte/Mt. Crested Butte, call the Crested Butte Mountain Resort (970–349–2333) or the Crested Butte Chamber of Commerce (970–349–6438).

Because this winter area is popular with everyone from cross-country skiers and snowshoers to snowmobilers, the area has a very large plowed parking area at the trailhead. The road to Irwin Lodge is popular with snowmobilers, so expect moderate to heavy use by individuals and tour groups. The Irwin Lodge provides transportation back and forth to the trailhead by grooming equipment for its overnight guests, so the road is usually extremely well packed, groomed, and maintained.

Whether you are day skiing or snowshoeing, after leaving the trailhead, the road takes you west. A deep ravine parallels your route on the left side for the first 2 miles. This is Coal Creek, and it provides chal-

Kebler Pass to Lake Irwin

Scale: 1:48,000 or 1.32" = 1 mile

START

FINISH

Road 12

Easy Route

Advanced Route

Intermediate Route

FR 826

lenging deep powder runs down to the creek bed. However if you get off onto one of the side paths that lead you to the bottom, the hike back up is rated as difficult. This same area is very popular with snowshoers who come equipped with snowboards. Hikes up above Coal Creek on both sides offer many side trails that will take you up to the top of deep powder ridges. Snowshoers and shoers with snowboards looking for "virgin deep powder" will find plenty in these uncrowded areas.

Directions at a glance

- From the parking area, the trail routes up County Road 12 west with Coal Creek on your left-hand side.

- At about 4.0 miles from the trailhead, the route branches off in three directions. The far left route takes you up over Kebler Pass. The far right route takes you to the Irwin Homestead. The middle route takes you to Lake Irwin and the Irwin Lodge.

- Take the middle trail marked as FR 826 and switchback uphill through heavy pines.

- Lake Irwin is 1.5 miles up FR 826. The Irwin Lodge sits across the lake on the north shore, approximately 0.5 mile farther up the road.

- To return, just follow the same route back down the hill and road to the trailhead, and enjoy the gentle glide/trek.

Alternate route

- At approximately 4.0 miles from the trailhead, take the trail to the right. It leads to the site of the old Irwin Homestead.

- This route is designed for skiers/shoers looking for a steeper climb. It goes approximately 1.0 mile to the town of Irwin.

- Out of Irwin the trail tracks northwest and goes down to Lake Irwin. Look for the Irwin Lodge on the north shore.

- To return, just follow the same route back down the hill and road to the trailhead, and enjoy the gentle glide/trek.

Approximately 4 miles up from the trailhead, the road splits in three different directions. The route to the extreme left continues on County Road 12 and will lead you up over the top of Kebler Pass, beyond Lost Lake, and eventually some 20 more miles down to the town of Paonia. Snowmobiles have groomed the trail, but it's a long hike or ski down to that trailhead—and a long way back! It's marked as the road to the Ruby–Anthracite Creek Valley.

The extreme right fork in the trail will take you—and most of the resident locals—to the Irwin Homestead area. The trail starts off as easy, quickly goes to an intermediate level, and finishes up with a difficult rating because it is steep. Most residents who live back in this area find that a high-powered snowmobile is the "transportation of choice" to commute back and forth to work. Although the trails are steep, they are well groomed and packed because of local snowmobile traffic.

If you reach the town of Irwin, visit the old abandoned Forest Queen Mine. From there head northwest through the conifers and you will come out at the edge of frozen Lake Irwin.

On the northeast shore of Lake Irwin is an old log cabin that can be easily accessed by everyone. If you're a movie buff, this cabin was the setting of the *Wilderness Family* series. It is maintained and is often occupied by visitors in the summer months.

The middle trail at the 4-mile mark is the one most skiers and snowshoers will want to take. It's a switchback trail that's marked as FR 826. It rates as intermediate because of the steeper climbs and leads northwest to Lake Irwin. It's about a 2-mile, mostly uphill, trek. It's well signed and traveled, and once you see the small lake nestled in the pines, you can easily follow the trail up to Irwin Lodge. Located on the north side above Irwin Lake, the Irwin Lodge is a magnificent, giant log structure that just about everyone considers a high mountain paradise spot hidden in the backwoods.

How to get there
Follow the signs out of downtown Crested Butte to Kebler Pass, County Road 12. (It's also the town's main street called Elk Avenue.) Follow County Road 12 approximately 2 miles to the winter parking area. Signs will tell you that NO VEHICLES ARE ALLOWED PAST THIS POINT.

Lottis Creek

Taylor Canyon, Gunnison, CO

Type of trail:	▬▬ ⬬
Distance:	12.2 miles
Terrain:	Steady climbs to trail's end and then fast glide or trek back to the trailhead.
Trail difficulty:	Easy/novice to intermediate
Surface quality:	Ungroomed but sometimes tracked by skiers/shoers.
Elevation:	Trailhead 9,000 feet at Lottis Creek Campground, ascends to above 10,100 feet
Time:	4 hours to full day
Avalanche danger:	Low for first 3.4 miles; increases to moderate after that
Food and facilities:	No facilities are found during the winter at the Lottis Creek Trail. There are plenty of restaurants, hotels, and grocery stores in Gunnison, including a newly opened City Market on Highway 135, less than 30 miles away. Seventeen miles back down the canyon at Almont, where County Road 742 cuts off from Highway 135, you'll find the 3-Rivers Resort and store (970–641–1303). Snacks, some dry goods, and gas are available, as are some winter cabins. You'll also find the Almont Resort (970–641–4009), with a restaurant and bar open for breakfast, lunch, and dinner. Sack lunches are also available and generously proportioned. Approximately 13 miles farther up Taylor Canyon from the Lottis Creek trailhead, you'll discover the Taylor Reservoir area where you'll find even more cross-country ski/snowshoe trails that start at the Taylor Park Trading Post (970–641–2555). Gas and dry goods groceries only are available during the winter at this popular summer resort area.

The trail begins approximately .10 mile above the campground area on County Road 742. The trailhead is well marked as Trail 428. There is a warning to visitors that the area is not open to motorized vehicles because it heads into a designated wilderness area. The trail heads southeast and up into the Fossil Ridge Wilderness Area. Approximately .75 mile from trailhead, the trail divides. The left fork, which heads east, is a route that is designated as Trail 758. This trail will lead you into the Union Canyon area. Although popular with summer hikers

and campers, the area has an often high avalanche danger rating. It's a 2.5-mile trail that should be avoided unless you've checked and been advised that the avalanche danger is low!

The safest and most scenic route is to take the right fork and stay on Trail 428. This trail heads in a more southern direction and meanders gently along South Lottis Creek. On some maps it's also called the Gunsight Trail, a name locals also use for it. The trail crosses the creek, and there are small- to medium-sized waterfall creek areas that are usually frozen solid and make for spectacular cascading ice sculptures and photo opportunities.

This trail begins with an easy or novice rating, but as it—and you—climb steadily uphill, it earns an intermediate rating. Skiers and shoers start at a narrow creek that climbs gently up into a broad but forested valley loaded with stands of conifers and aspen trees.

About 6.0 miles from the trailhead, you'll have climbed just over 2,900 feet, descended over 1,500 feet, gaining a total of about 1,400 feet in elevation. Even though the elevation increase is not great, this trail is a favorite for folks looking for a gentle but continuous climb upward. It's an easy walk back downhill if you're on snowshoes and a "fast glide" back down to the trailhead if you're on skis.

Directions at a glance

- Trailhead is marked as Trail 428. Head southeast from the campground.

- At about .75 mile look for Trail 758 that cuts off to the left and goes east.

- Continue steady climb along Trail 428, which runs parallel to South Lottis Creek.

- Trail continues a gentle climb for another 5.0 miles.

- To return go back on the same trail and enjoy the gentle downhill snowshoeing or skiing to the trailhead.

How to get there

From Gunnison go north on Highway 135 approximately 10 miles to the town of Almont. At Almont, make a right on County Road 742 up through Taylor Canyon, approximately 17 miles to the Lottis Creek Campground. The parking area is small, but it's usually plowed and open during most all of the winter.

Waunita Hot Springs

Gunnison, CO

Type of trail:	▬▬ ⬬
Also used by:	Snowmobilers
Distance:	16.0 miles
Terrain:	Steady climbs along Forest Routes to top of Pass for the beginner. More challenging and steeper ascents along the Intermediate route.
Trail difficulty:	Easy/novice to intermediate (difficult trails also available)
Surface quality:	Ungroomed but often tracked by skiers/shoers.
Elevation:	Trailhead 8,990 feet at Waunita Hot Springs, climbs to 10,300 feet at Waunita Pass
Time:	3 to 5 hours
Avalanche danger:	Low
Snowmobile use:	Medium
Food and facilities:	Gunnison lies about 25 miles south and west. Closest hotel/restaurant facilities are about 1 mile east of Gunnison in Tomichi Village. Call (970) 641–1131 for reservations at the Tomichi Village Best Western Hotel. Many other fine restaurants, overnight accommodations, grocery stores, etc. can also be found in Gunnison. Call the Gunnison County Chamber of Commerce at (970–641–1501) for brochures and information about winter skiing/shoeing and outdoor activities. For further information about Waunita Hot Springs and hours of operation, call (970) 641–1266.

everal snowshoeing or cross-country ski routes that range from easy to difficult are available in the area. The easy to intermediate route is the trail that is marked to Waunita Pass. Up about 0.5 mile from the Hot Springs Resort, the trail will be the road on your left. The first several miles of this trail are along a private road. Please stay on the marked pathway. Climbing from 8,900 feet at the trailhead to an elevation of 9,200 feet, the trail again forks about 2.0 miles in.

The shortest and easiest route up to the Waunita Pass at 10,300 feet is to stay to the left and continue up the old logging road that turns into Forest Route (FR) 763. This road winds its way and switchbacks through forest pockets of aspen and conifers, while paralleling Hot Springs Creek. The climb is gentle but constant, ideal for beginners looking for an easy

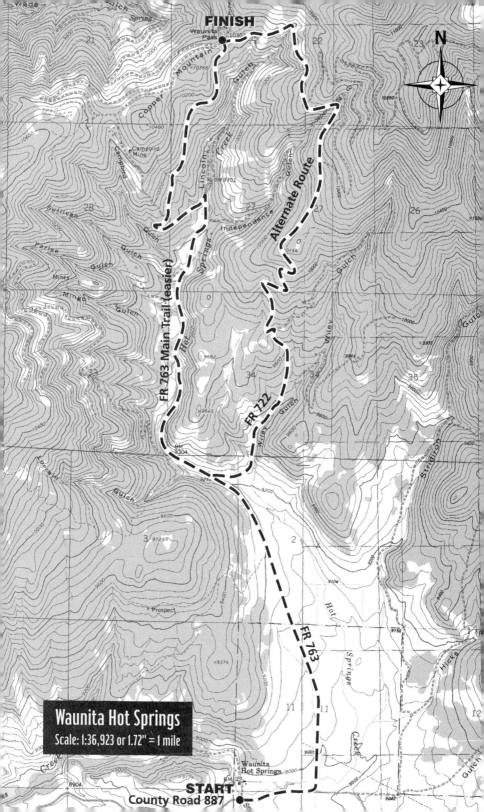

FINISH
Waunita
Pass

N

FR 763 Main Trail (easier)

Alternate Route

FR 722

FR 763

Waunita Hot Springs
Scale: 1:36,923 or 1.72" = 1 mile

Waunita
Hot Springs

START
County Road 887

route. All along the trail, pockets of open water can be found along the creek in the early winter and early spring months. The warm water often disappears back into the ground but eventually comes out and feeds the hot springs back at the Waunita Hot Springs Resort.

If you are looking for a more challenging route, take the FR 722 at the fork, just over 2.0 miles from the trailhead. The route cuts off to the right, goes about 0.5 mile and then cuts back to the left. Keep following the route to your left, and you'll come out at the top of Waunita Pass. This route is for intermediate skiers and snowshoers, and the climb to the pass is steeper and narrower. This trail parallels Wiley Gulch and provides an invigorating, but not too challenging, 4.6-mile route to the top of Waunita Pass.

If you are a beginning skier or snowshoer, take the easier route at the trail juncture of FR 763 and FR 722 to the left. It's about 1.75 miles up to Independence Gulch, and then another 0.5 mile to Lincoln Creek, where the trail does a hairpin switchback to the left. Then it's a 0.25-mile climb to Campbird Gulch, where the trail hairpins back to the right and continues climbing. From here, it's less than 1.5 miles to the top of the pass.

If you are either a novice or intermediate skier/shoer, you find that at the top of Waunita Pass you can now loop back down by crossing over to either the easy or intermediate route back to the trailhead. FR 763 is the easier trail, while FR 722 is the intermediate level trail. Both are marked with wood signs at the top of the pass.

Challenging glade skiing is available on the north side of Waunita Pass, but the routes are recommended for intermediate and advance skiers only. It's easy to hike and ski down, but the trip back up is rated as difficult on most of these side trails.

The Waunita Hot Springs Resort is a very popular summer and winter destination. The hot springs are open year-round to the public. However, in the winter months all of the lodging and restaurant facilities are for on-site guests only. No walk-in reservations for meals or lodging are accepted. But for $8.00 per person, it's an excellent idea to put a swimming suit in your car or daypack. The hot springs and pool facilities are a great way to unwind and relax tired muscles after a day in the backcountry.

How to get there

From Gunnison go approximately 16.0 miles east on Highway 50 to the Waunita Hot Springs turnoff at County Road 887. Turnoff will be on your left and is well marked. Go approximately 9.0 miles northeast to the Waunita Hot Springs Resort. Closed gate on the roadway is a Forest Service closure in winter months. Park along roadside by the resort, but do not block the road or access area. Ski/snowshoe trail begins there at the closed gate, but official trailhead is approximately 0.5 mile past the Waunita Hot Springs Resort.

Directions at a glance

- Trail route begins at Forest Service gate/road closure. Go 0.5 mile east to the trailhead.

- Go left, heading north on the road. Stay on the road, until it turns into Forest Route (FR) 763.

- Continue approximately 2.0 miles from the trailhead and look for cutoff to FR 722. Fork to the left continues up FR 763. This is the easiest route.

- It's another 5.25 miles to the Waunita Pass summit.

- Come back down the same way with gentle downhill ski/shoeing course, or head east to FR 722 for more challenging downhill back 4.6 miles until you again intersect FR 763.

- At this juncture it's a short 2.0 miles back downhill to the trailhead.

Alternate route

- At approximately 2.0 miles from the trailhead, look for Forest Route (FR) 722 sign. The trail will cut off to your right.

- Go right and enjoy a steeper climb on a loop that will meet back up at the top of Waunita Pass, approximately 4.6 miles from this juncture.

- FR 722 goes about 0.5 mile and then forks. Take left fork and continue to take the left fork junctures.

- FR 722 comes out at the top of Waunita Pass.

- Turn around and go back the same way for a more challenging route, or intersect FR 763 at Waunita Pass and take the easy/novice road back to the trailhead.

North Pole Hut

San Juan Mountains, Ridgway, CO

Type of trail:	▬▬ 🥾
Distance:	16.0 to 22.0 miles
Terrain:	Beginning trail follows flat and level road, followed by moderately challenging climbs and descents all the way to the Hut. Trail is long, often not well marked, and requires advanced navigation/map reading skills.
Trail difficulty:	Intermediate to advanced ski/snowshoe abilities; advanced navigation skills required
Surface quality:	Ungroomed and not often tracked by skiers/shoers.
Elevation:	Trailhead at 8,300 feet and the hut at 9,999 feet
Time:	8 or more hours each way
Avalanche danger:	Low to moderate. Areas where avalanche terrain may be encountered can be avoided.
Food and facilities:	Because of the remoteness of the North Pole Hut, winter users are advised to carry plenty of lightweight high-energy snack foods, 2 liters of water, and emergency bivouac supplies, including a shovel, sacs or tarps, and no-cook food supplies. Grocery stores, hotels, and restaurant facilities can be found in the Ridgway area. If you stay overnight in Ridgway, make sure you get up and plan for a very early start. On the trail by first light is the best suggestion! For more information about the hut system or guide availability, contact Mike Turrin or Joe Ryan at San Juan Hut Systems. You can call them (970–728–6935) or check out information about all of their hut systems on the Web: www.telluridegateway.com/sjhuts.

The San Juan mountain range is the largest in the state of Colorado and is a favorite for summertime mountaineers, rock climbers, mountain bikers, and hikers. In the wintertime it's a popular area for everyone from downhill and telemark skiers to snowshoers and even ice climbers. The problem is that the San Juans are extremely steep and craggy, making them majestic in their beauty but difficult for backcountry skiers and shoers to access. The 14,000-foot ridgelike peaks tower far above tree-line areas and offer very few skiable passes. Compound this with the fact that the avalanche danger is often high.

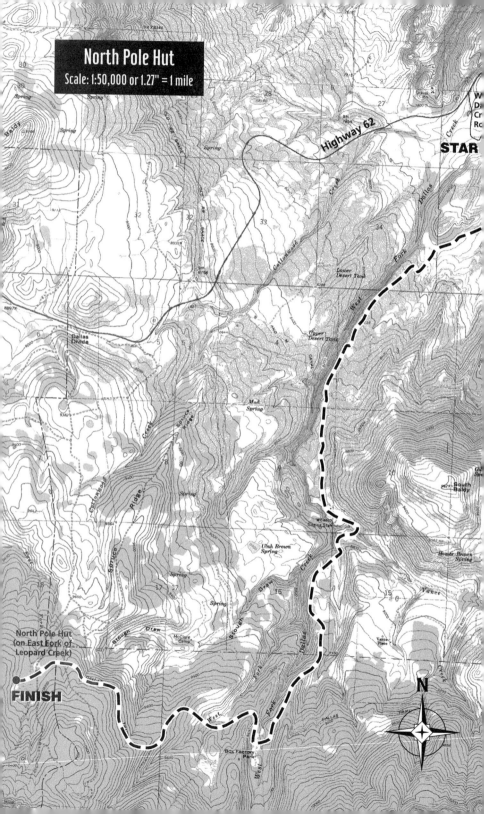

In the mid-1980s, two residents of Telluride, Colorado, decided the time had come to overcome the natural difficulties posed by the terrain. Mike Turrin and Joe Ryan, avid backcountry skiers, decided to build a hut system and let the rest of the skiing and snowshoeing world have access to some of the most scenic areas in the nation.

The two visionaries went to work and linked the 30-plus mile stretch from Telluride to Ridgway with five huts, placing the structures along old logging roads and trails. The routes to and from the trailheads to the huts are designed for intermediate skier ability, while the routes from hut to hut are more taxing and should be undertaken by more experienced and advanced skiers.

The North Pole Hut is remarkable for its incredible remoteness, which may appeal to backcountry skiers who want to feel they're in the midst of nature's wild and view the surrounding mountain range the way it has looked for millions of years. Near the North Pole Hut, which is located just outside the border of the Mount Sneffels Wilderness Area, skiers and snowshoers will not hear any mechanized vehicles or other sounds, save their own skis or shoes moving on the snow.

The North Pole Hut is located in a meadow on the East Fork of Leopard Creek. Because it is so remote, there will generally not be any day skiers in the area. You have the trees and the mountains and the views of Hayden Peak and North Pole Peak to yourself. When avalanche dangers are low, ski mountaineers and snowshoers can try the north ridge of Hayden.

Photo by Tari and Andy Lightbody

If fresh, deep powder is your love, you can enjoy the ridges and slopes below the tree lines. Or if you prefer an easier pace and mellow ski touring is what you love best, there are old roads and trails south of the hut.

Parties are advised to be under way on the trail by no later than sunrise. It is likely that they will still be on the trail until nearly dark or possibly even after dark. The trail is not overly steep, but it is very long, and advanced route-finding skills are necessary. A compass, topo map, and even a handheld GPS receiver are highly recommended. Everyone in the party should carry headlamps and flashlights with extra batteries. This trek to the North Pole Hut is going to require you to give great attention to your maps, compass, San Juan Hut System's instructions, tree blaises, tree scalp marks, metal flags, and signs. Unless you are able to handle the long trek and navigate extremely well in the woods, you may want to consider hiring a guide to lead you.

From the trailhead for the first 6.5 miles, follow the roads and very detailed instructions obtained from the San Juan Hut Systems until you intersect the Dallas Trail 200. Head west on the Dallas Trail into the National Forest following very specific "blue-and-silver" diamond signs that are posted on the trees. The route along the Dallas Trail 200 is not well marked by the Forest Service hence the numerous diamond signs and red flag markers!

The route along the Dallas Trail 200 goes up, down, and along the sides of hills to the west for approximately 4.2 miles through groves of conifers, aspen, and Gambel's oak. There are also open meadows, treeless hillsides, and always-spectacular views. The last 0.25 to 0.5 mile of the route to the hut is off the Dallas Trail, and the hut is located in a very secluded area north alongside an open meadow.

The hut, which originally started out as a yurt but was enclosed a couple of years ago, comes complete with padded bunks that will sleep up to eight visitors. Other amenities include a propane cook stove, propane lamp, propane, wood stove, firewood, axes, snow scoops, simple outdoor toilets, and all necessary kitchen facilities. Melting the outside snow provides your water supply. Reservations are required, and the cost is $22 per person, per night. Representatives from the San Juan Hut System will meet with you in advance of your journey to go over maps and routes and update you on the latest snow conditions.

How to get there

From Montrose head south on Highway 550 approximately 20 miles to the town of Ridgway. Follow the signs toward the Telluride Ski Resort on Highway 62 for about 7 miles. Pass Forest Road (FR) 7 to Dallas Creek. Next Forest Road is FR 9 and the sign says WEST DALLAS CREEK. Make a left and go south on West Dallas Creek Road. The road passes through the Double RL ranch. Depending on the time of year and road conditions, it may be possible to shuttle loads in 1 or 2 miles, drop them, and return your vehicle to the road head. Park your vehicle only at the road head or run the severe risk of having it snowed in!

Directions at a glance

- From the trailhead at the West Dallas Creek Road, head south for approximately 6.5 miles. Begin no later than sunrise.
- Intersect the Dallas Trail 200 and make a right, heading west. Road ends and trail becomes narrow.
- Watch for and closely follow blue-and-silver diamond and red flag markers.
- Go west approximately 1.0 mile, and you'll intercept a wider dirt road/4-by-4 vehicle trail.
- Turn left, heading southwest and follow the road for 0.5 mile.
- Look for trail signs and diamond markers. Road will continue southwest, but you'll make a right back onto the Dallas Trail 200.
- Dallas Trail heads west, then northwest for 1.25 miles. Look for the wide jeep trail running north and south, intersecting the Dallas Trail.
- Continue west on the Dallas Trail 200 till it ends. Look for the meadow down below about 0.25 mile west.
- Drop down into the meadow to the west, and North Pole Hut lies across the meadow and about 0.10 mile up the hillside.
- To return, get an early start and follow the same route back to the trailhead and where you parked your vehicle.

Lizard Head Pass

Lizard Head Pass, Telluride, CO

Type of trail:	▬▬▬ ⬤
Also used by:	Snowmobilers
Distance:	5.5 miles to Railroad trestle and back—easy.
	7.5 miles to Lake Fork Canyon and back—easy to intermediate.
	3.75 miles from trailhead to Railroad trestle, and then to end of trail along the North Trout Lake Road—easy but must leave shuttle vehicle.
	7.5 miles from trailhead to Railroad trestle, then to end of trail along the North Trout Lake Road and return to trailhead.
Terrain:	Trail follows an old railroad bed and is gradual and gentle for first 2.75 miles. At the split, the trail to the right has moderate climbs to the trail end. The trail to the left continues with a road route and follows a gentle, flat course to the north end of Trout Lake.
Trail difficulty:	Easy to intermediate
Surface quality:	Ungroomed but usually well tracked by skiers/shoers.
Elevation:	Trailhead at Lizard Head Pass elevation 10,200 feet; trail end elevation 9,700 feet near outlet of Trout Lake.
Time:	3 to 5 hours
Snowmobile use:	Moderate
Food and facilities:	Facilities are sparse in the area, and gas, ski/shoe equipment, and groceries are best obtained before leaving Telluride. Lodging is best found in Telluride—where it is expensive—or back in Ridgway, where hotel and motel accommodations are much more reasonable in price. A few small towns can be found between Telluride and Lizard Head Pass, but most of these cater to summer visitors and are closed for the winter months. At the top of Lizard Head Pass is the summit sign, explaining the historical significance of the pass, and Forest Service provided toilets.

The trail begins at Lizard Head Pass and follows the old Denver and Rio Grande Railroad bed. The tracks have long since disappeared, but the railroad bed is still there and provides an easy-to-follow route from the pass back down through Lizard Head Meadows. From

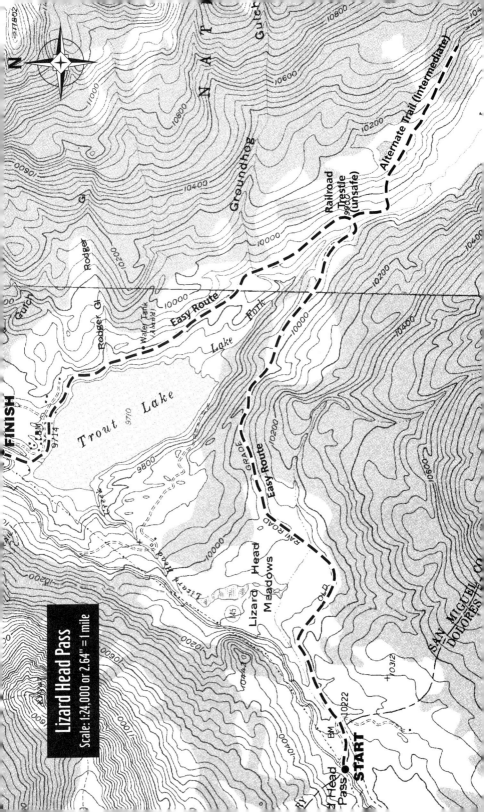

there the trail swings to the east and sidehills for about 1.0 mile. There are good views to the north of Trout Lake as you ski or snowshoe in and out of timber stands. Continue along the trail until it reaches the North Trout Lake Road. This area is popular with snowmobilers, so expect to find some noise and traffic.

The trail crosses over the Lake Fork Creek, and there is an old railroad trestle at the Trout Lake crossing. Although this is a scenic and somewhat historic view, the trestle is posted and chained off as being very unsafe. Forest officials are very concerned that the weight of snow and people could collapse it. If you're a beginner, this is a good place to turn around and hike or ski back to the trailhead.

The trail splits after the Lake Fork crossing, and you're about 2.75 miles in from the Lizard Head Pass trailhead. The most scenic trip is 1.9 or 2.0 miles up the Lake Fork Canyon, but here is where the trail turns from an easy to an intermediate level. At the railroad trestle, turn right and head southeast—following the drainage. Trail signs will head you south and southeast and will be marked as the trail to Lake Hope. It's advised that you stay well to the north—or left—of the meadow to avoid avalanche paths. Treeless slopes and stunted and toppled trees on the opposite slopes attest to the force of avalanches that have come through the area in previous winters.

The other trail at the Lake Fork crossing will head northwest (left), following the North Trout Lake Road. After a fresh snow, it's a gentle

Photo by Roy Kasting ©, courtesy of O₂ Productions, www.westernlight.com

Directions at a glance

- From the trailhead at Lizard Head Pass, follow the old railroad bed east 0.25 mile.

- Trail turns northeast for 0.50 mile and opens up above large meadow.

- Continue on the trail that traverses the side of a hill for another 1.5 miles till reaching an old and unstable railroad trestle bridge. *Stay off the trestle—it is very unsafe.*

- Go 0.25 mile past the bridge and the trail will come to a T-shaped intersection.

- Intermediate and advanced skiers/shoers may want to take the trail to the right, heading southeast deeper into the backcountry toward Lake Hope.

- Beginners can turn around at the T-shaped intersection and ski the approximately 2.75 miles back to the trailhead.

- To continue at the intersection, beginners can make a left onto the North Trout Lake Road. It's plowed and sometimes spotty, but a gentle glide all across the east side of Trout Lake.

- At the end of your ski/shoe tour, follow the same route back to the trailhead.

downhill hike or glide for about 1.0 mile along the east side of Trout Lake. It's often plowed quickly after a snowstorm, gets a lot of snow-mobile use, and can be spotty. Follow the North Trout Lake Road, which will bring you out at the north end of the lake. Here the road connects back up to Highway 145. You can either reverse the trail at this point, or pick up that well-placed "shuttle vehicle" here at the Trout Lake junction.

During windy and stormy weather, Lizard Head Pass can be very uncomfortable. There are a few trees at the pass and trailhead area, but it's a lot of open hillside and meadows. The farther you progress, the fewer trees there are to serve as windbreaks and help block or break up the often "cutting" winds.

How to get there

From Telluride drive south on State Highway 145 for 15 miles to Lizard Head Pass. Park on the side road to the east, or left side, of the pass or on the turnout that's located several hundred yards north of the pass. Plowed parking is often difficult to find right after heavy snows.

Appendix

U.S. Forest Service Offices/Avalanche Information

Arapaho–Roosevelt National Forest
240 West Prospect Road
Ft. Collins, CO 80526-2098
970–498–1100

Grand Mesa, Uncompahgre, and
Gunnison National Forests
2250 Highway 50
Delta, CO 81416-8723
970–874–6600

Pike and San Isabel National
Forests
1920 Valley Drive
Pueblo, CO 81008
719–545–8737

Rocky Mountain Regional Office
740 Sims
Lakewood, CO 80225
303–275–5350

San Juan National Forest
701 Camino Del Rio
Room 301
Durango, CO 81301
970–247–4874

White River National Forest
9th and Grand
P.O. Box 948
Glenwood Springs, CO 81602
970–945–2521

Avalanche Information Centers

Aspen: 970–920–1664
Fort Collins: 970–482–0457
Frisco: 970–668–0600
Front Range: 303–275–5360
Vail: 970–827–5687

Hut/Cabin Reservations

For the Lake Agnes Cabin call the Colorado State Forest State Park at 800–678–CAMP.
From Denver call 303–470–1144.

Emergency Numbers in Park

Park Office: 970–723–8366
Jackson County Sheriff: 970–723–4242

For Lindley and Tagert Memorial Huts and Friends Hut call the Tenth Mountain Division Hut Association at 970–925–5755.
USFS Aspen Avalanche Forecast number is 970–920–1664.

Colorado Mountain Club–Boulder Chapter
825 South Broadway, Suite 40
Boulder, CO 80303
303–554–7688; 303–441–2436

Rocky Mountain National Park
General park information: 970–586–1206
For fee permits call park headquarters at 970–586–2371 for east side tour.
Call Kawuneeche Visitor Center near Grand Lake at 970–627–3471 for fee permits for west side trips.
Park headquarters' number is 970–586–1399.

Colorado Avalanche Information Center for daily updates: 303–482–0457 for Cameron Pass; 303–275–5360 for Clear Creek, Loveland.

Breckenridge: Boreas Pass Section House, Francie's Cabin, call Tenth Mountain Division Hut Association at 970–925–5775.

Copper Mountain: Janet's Cabin, call Tenth Mountain Division Hut Association at 970–925–5775.

Vail Pass: Shrine Mountain Inn, call Tenth Mountain Division Hut Association at 970–925–5775.

Tenth Mountain Division Hut, call Tenth Mountain Division Hut Association at 970–925–5775.

Leadville: Tennessee Pass Cookhouse, Dinner Yurt, Call 719–486–1750 or 719–486–8114.

Telluride: North Pole Yurt, call 970–728–6935.

Crested Butte: Washington Gulch-Elkton Cabin, call Adventures to the Edge Limited at 970–349–5219.

Chambers of Commerce

Aspen: 970–925–1940

Breckenridge: 970–453–6018

Copper Mountain: 800–530–3099

Crested Butte: 970–344–6438/
800–545–4505

Estes Park for Rocky Mountain
National Park: 970–586–4431/
800–44–ESTES

Fairplay: 970–836–3410

Fort Collins for Cameron Pass area:
970–482–3746

Frisco: 970–668–5800

Glenwood Springs: 970–945–6589

Granby: 970–887–2311

Grand Junction for Powderhorn:
970–242–3214

Keystone: 970–668–5800

Leadville: 719–486–3900

Meeker Park, Front Range:
970–878–5510

Montrose: 970–249–5000/
800–873–0244

Nederland, Front Range:
303–258–3936

Ouray: 970–325–4746/800–228–1876

Salida: 719–539–2068

Steamboat Springs: 970–879–0880

Telluride: 970–728–3041

Vail: 970–949–5189

Winter Park, Front Range:
970–726–4118

Nordic Centers

Breckenridge Area

Breckenridge Nordic Center
1200 Ski Hill Road
P.O. Box 1776
Breckenridge, CO 80424
970–453–6855
23 km of groomed, double-set track

Copper Mountain

Copper Mountain Cross-Country
Center
P.O. Box 3001-D
Copper Mountain, CO 80443
970–968–2882, ext
6342/800–458–8386, ext 5
25 km of groomed trails
Trail pass $10, seniors $8.00, over
70 and under 5 are free, season
pass $60
Open November–April

Crested Butte Area

Crested Butte Mountain Resort
P.O. Box A
Mount Crested Butte, CO 81225
970–349–2333/800–544–8488

Crested Butte Nordic Center
620 2nd Street
Crested Butte, CO 81224
970–349–1707
20 km of groomed track

Eldora Ski Area

Eldora Nordic Center
P.O. Box 1697
Nederland, CO 80466-1697
303–440–8700
45 km of groomed track
Trail fee $10, seniors $7.00

Nordic Centers (continued)

Frisco Ski Area

Frisco Nordic Center
P.O. Box 532
Frisco, CO 80443
970–668–0866
35 km of groomed trails

Glenwood Springs Area

Ski Sunlight
10901 Road 117
Glenwood Springs, CO 81601
970–945–7491/800–445–7931
10 km of groomed trails

Grand Junction Area

Grand Mesa Nordic Council
P.O. Box 3077
Grand Junction, CO 81502
970–434–9753/970–434–4609

Powderhorn Resort
P.O. Box 370
Mesa, CO 81643
970–268–5700

Keystone Area

Keystone Cross-Country Center
P.O. Box 38
Keystone, CO 80435
303–468–4275/800–451–5930
46 km of groomed trails
Open Thanksgiving to Easter

Leadville Area

Piney Creek Nordic Center
P.O. Box 223
Leadville, CO 80461
719–486–1750
24 km of groomed trails

Monarch Ski Area

Monarch Ski Resort
#1 Powder Place
U.S. Highway 50
Monarch, CO 81227
719–539–3573/800–332–3668
3.2 km of groomed trails

Powderhorn Ski Area

Powderhorn Resort
P.O. Box 370
Mesa, CO 81643
970–268–5700/800–241–6997
12 km of groomed trails

Purgatory Area

Purgatory Nordic Center
3001 West 3rd Avenue
Durango, CO 81301
970–247–9000, ex 114/970–385–2114
16 km of groomed trails

Rocky Mountain National Park Area

The Grand Lake Touring Center
P.O. Box 590
Grand Lake, CO 80447
303–627–8008
20 km of groomed trails

Steamboat Springs Area

Howelson Ski Area
P.O. Box 775088
Steamboat Springs, CO 80477
970–879–8499
10 km of groomed trails

Steamboat Springs Ski Touring Center
P.O. Box 772297
Steamboat Springs, CO 80477
970–879–8180
30 km groomed track

Vista Verde Guest and Ski Touring
Ranch
P.O. Box 465X
Steamboat Springs, CO 80477
800–526–7433
30 km of groomed trails

Telluride Area

Telluride Nordic Center
P.O. Box 11155
565 Mountain Village Boulevard
Telluride, CO 81435
970–728–6900/800–525–3455
30 km of groomed trails

Vail Area

Beaver Creek Cross-Country
Ski Center
Vail Resort
P.O. Box 7
Vail, CO 81658
970–845–5313

Vail Associates
P.O. Box 7
Vail, CO 81658
970–926–3029

Vail Golf Course
458-X Vail Valley Drive
Vail, CO 81657
970–949–5750

Winter Park Area

Devil's Thumb Ranch by Winter
Park
P.O. Box 1364
Winter Park, CO 80482
970–726–5632
105 km of groomed trails

Snow Mountain Ranch Nordic
Center
P.O. Box 169
Winter Park, CO 80482
970–726–4628/970–887–2152
100 km of groomed trails
Open November to mid-April

Silver Creek Nordic Center
P.O. Box 1110
Silver Creek, CO 80446
970–887–3384; Denver:
303–629–1020/800–448–9458
40 km of groomed trails

Colorado Ski Country USA represents twenty-six ski areas in Colorado, serves as an information clearinghouse, supplies a ninety-six-page detailed directory of Colorado ski areas free of charge. Write to CSCUSA, 1560 Broadway, Suite 1440, Denver, CO 80202; or call 303–837–0793. Alto supplies twenty-four-hour snow report line at 303–031 SNOW.

Colorado Cross-Country Ski Association
P.O. Box 1336
Winter Park, CO 80482
800–869–4560

Colorado Cross-Country Ski Association
P.O. Box 1292
Kremmling, CO 80459
800–869–4560

About the Authors

TARI LIGHTBODY

A dedicated researcher and writer, Tari pens articles for local, regional, and national magazines, and has earned contributing credits for a host of national and international books. Her latest writings include personally authored books for publication in 1999 in the romance, mystery, and intrigue lines.

Even while writing all of these books and articles, Tari is always "Mom" to her children—Daniel, Jeffrey, Matthew, and Jennifer.

ANDY LIGHTBODY

A lifelong outdoorsman, Andy loves to share his knowledge of the outdoors through articles, books, and broadcasts. His written works have been published by Petersen Publishing Company, Challenge Publications, *Consumer Guide,* and *Consumer Digest.* In addition, through broadcasts on CBS Radio, CNBC-TV, and FOX-TV, he has continued to report about the myriad outdoor recreational opportunities, and the importance of conserving the environment for today and for future generations.

Today, Andy is a regional correspondent for *Fishing & Hunting News Magazine,* the host of the radio program *Colorado's Outdoor Minutes,* and is a regular contributor to many outdoor recreation magazines. Even while writing and broadcasting, Andy remains a dedicated "Dad."

Summer isn't the only time to go outside and play!

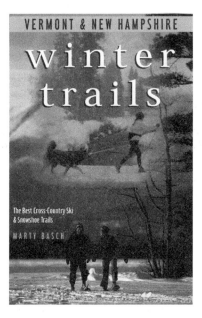

Take the guesswork out of finding the perfect trail with this brand-new series. Written for outdoor enthusiasts of all skill levels, our guidebooks provide you with all the information you need to experience first-hand the beauty of America's cross-country and snowshoeing trails.

Also in this series:
Winter Trails™ Vermont and New Hampshire

Come out and play with The Globe Pequot Press!

FOR OTHER BOOKS ON OUTDOOR RECREATION, CHECK YOUR LOCAL BOOKSTORE OR CONTACT:
The Globe Pequot Press • P.O. Box 833 • Old Saybrook, CT 06475
PH: 800–243–0495 • www.globe-pequot.com